# RETHINKING BRITAIN

"In the face of climate and social breakdown we urgently need new public policy ideas. *Rethinking Britain* has them in wonderful, creative and powerful bucketfuls. It's a must-read for anyone who wants to reclaim Britain for the many, not the few."
*Paul Chatterton, University of Leeds*

"Brexit has displaced other policy issues, so this review of a variety of progressive proposals, with its helpful jargon buster, is a very valuable reminder of what needs to be done."
*Ron Smith, Birkbeck, University of London*

# RETHINKING BRITAIN

## Policy Ideas for the Many

Edited by Sue Konzelmann, Susan Himmelweit,
Jeremy Smith and John Weeks

First published in Great Britain in 2019 by

Policy Press
University of Bristol
1-9 Old Park Hill
Bristol
BS2 8BB
UK
t: +44 (0)117 954 5940
pp-info@bristol.ac.uk
www.policypress.co.uk

North America office:
Policy Press
c/o The University of Chicago Press
1427 East 60th Street
Chicago, IL 60637, USA
t: +1 773 702 7700
f: +1 773 702 9756
sales@press.uchicago.edu
www.press.uchicago.edu

British Library Cataloguing in Publication Data
A catalogue record for this book is available from the British Library.

Library of Congress Cataloging-in-Publication Data
A catalog record for this book has been requested.

ISBN 978-1-4473-5252-5 paperback
ISBN 978-1-4473-5253-2 ePub
ISBN 978-1-4473-5255-6 ePdf

The right of Sue Konzelmann, Susan Himmelweit, Jeremy Smith and John Weeks to be identified as the editors of this work has been asserted by them in accordance with the Copyright, Designs and Patents Act 1988.

Cover design by Liron Gilenberg
Printed and bound in Great Britain by TJ International, Padstow
Policy Press uses environmentally responsible print partners

# Contents

# Contents

# List of tables and figures

## Tables

## Figures

# The contributors

**Pauline Allen** is Professor of Health Services Organisation at the London School of Hygiene and Tropical Medicine, London, UK.

**Antonio Andreoni** is Senior Lecturer in Economics at SOAS University of London, UK, and Research Director of the Anti-Corruption Evidence Research Consortium (ACE).

**Dean Baker** is Senior Economist at the Center for Economic and Policy Research, Washington, DC, USA.

**Bruno Bonizzi** is Lecturer in Political Economy at the University of Winchester, UK.

**Ha-Joon Chang** is Reader in Economics at the University of Cambridge, UK and Council Member of the Progressive Economy Forum, London, UK.

**Jennifer Churchill** is Lecturer in Economics at Kingston University, UK.

**Hulya Dagdeviren** is Professor of Economic Development at the University of Hertfordshire, UK.

**Jerome De Henau** is Senior Lecturer in Economics at the Open University, UK and Co-chair for Policy at the UK Women's Budget Group, London, UK.

**Simon Deakin** is Professor of Law and Director of the Centre for Business Research at the University of Cambridge, UK.

**Keith D. Ewing** is Professor of Public Law at King's College London, UK and President of the Institute of Employment Rights, Liverpool, UK.

**Marc Fovargue-Davies** is a Research Associate at the Cambridge Centre for Business Research, UK.

**Ian Gough** is Visiting Professor at the Centre for the Analysis of Social Exclusion (CASE), London School of Economics and Political Science, UK.

**John Grahl** is Professor of European Integration in the Human Resources Department at Middlesex University, UK.

**Francis Green** is Professor of Work and Education Economics at UCL Institute of Education, UK, and co-author with David Kynaston of *Engines of Privilege. Britain's Private School Problem* (Bloomsbury, 2019).

**Stephany Griffith-Jones** is Financial Markets Director, Initiative for Policy Dialogue (IPD), Columbia University, USA, Emeritus Professorial Fellow, Institute of Development Studies (IDS), Sussex University, UK, and Council Member of the Progressive Economy Forum, London, UK.

**Colin Haslam** is Professor of Accounting & Finance at Queen Mary University of London, UK. He is a member of the Foundational Economy collective and a contributor to *Foundational Economy: The Infrastructure of Everyday Life* (Manchester University Press, 2018).

**John Hendy QC** is Chair of the Institute of Employment Rights, Liverpool, UK, Vice-Chair of the International Centre for Trade Union Rights (ICTUR), Joint Secretary to the United Campaign for the Repeal of Anti Trade Union Laws, and Standing Counsel to several trade union organisations.

**Susan Himmelweit** is Emeritus Professor of Economics at the Open University, UK, Coordinator of the Policy Advisory

Group of the Women's Budget Group, London, UK, and Council Member of the Progressive Economy Forum, London, UK.

**Leslie Huckfield** was MP for Nuneaton from 1967 to 1983, Under Secretary of State at the Department of Trade and Industry from 1976 until 1979 and MEP for Merseyside East from 1984 to 1989. He is a Lecturer at the Glasgow School for Business and Society at Glasgow Caledonian University, UK.

**Sue Konzelmann** is Reader in Management at Birkbeck, University of London, UK, Council Member of the Progressive Economy Forum, London, UK, Research Associate of the Cambridge Centre for Business Research, UK, and Co-Executive Editor of the *Cambridge Journal of Economics*. She is also author of *Austerity* (Polity, 2019).

**David Kynaston** is a professional historian, currently an honorary professor at Kingston University, UK, and co-author with Francis Green of *Engines of Privilege. Britain's Private School Problem* (Bloomsbury, 2019).

**Stewart Lansley** is Visiting Fellow at the University of Bristol, UK. He is the author of *A Sharing Economy* (Policy Press, 2016).

**Jane Lethbridge** is Co-Director of the Centre for Research on Employment and Work (CREW) at the University of Greenwich, UK, and contributes to the Public Services International Research Unit (PSIRU), Business Faculty, University of Greenwich, UK.

**John Marlow** works in the financial sector. Regrettably, he feels it necessary to use a pseudonym.

**Liz Marr** is Acting Pro-Vice Chancellor for Students at the Open University, UK, President of the European Association of Distance Education, Chair of the UK Action on Access Forum, and Executive Member of the Universities Association for Lifelong Learning.

**Duncan McCann** is Research Fellow at City, University of London, UK and Researcher at the New Economics Foundation, UK.

**Johnna Montgomerie** is Reader in International Political Economy at King's College London, UK, and Council Member of the Progressive Economy Forum, London, UK.

**Richard Murphy** is Professor of Practice in International Political Economy at City University, London, UK, and Director of Tax Research UK, Ely. He is a non-executive director of Cambridge Econometrics, UK.

**Natalya Naqvi** is Assistant Professor in International Political Economy at the London School of Economics and Political Science, UK.

**Özlem Onaran** is Professor of Economics and Director of Greenwich Political Economy Research Centre, University of Greenwich, UK.

**Dan O'Neill** is Associate Professor in Ecological Economics at the University of Leeds, UK, and co-author (with Rob Dietz) of *Enough Is Enough: Building a Sustainable Economy in a World of Finite Resources* (Routledge, 2013).

**Kate Pickett** is Professor of Epidemiology in the Department of Health Sciences at the University of York, UK, and is the University's Research Champion for Justice and Equality.

**Howard Reed** is the Director of Landman Economics, Colchester, UK.

**Alan Shipman** is Lecturer in Economics at the Open University, UK.

**Jeremy Smith** is Co-Director of Prime Economics, London, UK.

**Mary-Ann Stephenson** is Director of the Women's Budget Group, London, UK.

**Beth Stratford** is Fellow of the New Economics Foundation, a guest lecturer and PhD researcher at the University of Leeds, UK, with a focus on housing and ecological economics.

**Jeff Tan** is Associate Professor in Political Economy at the Institute for the Study of Muslim Civilisations, Aga Khan University, Pakistan.

**Jan Toporowski** is Professor of Economics and Finance at SOAS University of London, UK.

**John Weeks** is Professor Emeritus, SOAS University of London, UK, Associate of Prime Economics, London, UK, and Coordinator of the Progressive Economy Forum, London, UK.

# Foreword

*Patrick Allen*

As the founder and Chair of the Progressive Economy Forum, I am delighted to support the launch of this excellent book. *Rethinking Britain* is a collection of essays designed to cover major policy ideas for a complete redesign of the UK economy. Goodness knows that such a project is needed.

The UK has been subject to a disastrous economic experiment since the election of the Thatcher government in 1979. The 'neoliberal' agenda involved privatisation of state assets, restricting trade union powers, abolition of capital controls, reducing tax on high earners and deregulation to set business free from the alleged constraints of red tape.

Our manufacturing industry shrank and many areas became economically depressed as factories closed. They have remained that way in the absence of any proper regional or industrial policy. The economy became more focused on services, especially financial services.

Growth in the economy never matched up to that achieved in the 'Golden Age of Economics' from 1950 to 1975. There were periods of mass unemployment and volatility. Inequality increased. The de-regulated financial sector expanded and drove a huge increase in debt and mortgages which led directly to the 2008 crash.

Post-crash our public debt and deficit rose as GDP fell by 6%, government tax receipts dried up and spending on benefits rose as unemployment increased. A Keynesian-inspired stimulus package in 2009 enabled a recovery to start but this was halted in 2010 by the Conservative-led coalition government. Their remedy of austerity to reduce public debt by cuts in public spending has predictably resulted in the slowest recovery from recession since records began.

Public debt as a percentage of GDP is now higher in 2019 than it was in 2010. Real wages have incredibly still not recovered to pre-crash levels. Child poverty and homelessness have rocketed. The resulting unhappiness and financial insecurity of many citizens led to the Brexit vote which has paralysed our politics for three years and if implemented will make things still worse.

The neoliberal experiment has had its day and has failed to bring prosperity and stability. However, it will only end with the election of a progressive government dedicated to ending austerity and implementing sustainable policies to rebuild the economy.

So what exactly will that entail? That is where this book come in.

The contributors cover a vast range of necessary policy areas and ideas, not least those concerned with managing the economy to maximise its potential. They include the concept of universal basic income, nationalisation of utilities and railways, the management of public debt for investment, the role of unions and labour law, regional and industrial policy, and the reduction of wealth and gender inequality.

There is so much to be done, but what is heartening is the sheer energy and wealth of ideas coming from progressive thinkers to fill the vacuum left by the failure of neoliberalism.

Inevitably this involves significant strategic planning and spending by the state to invest in our future which was a feature of the highly successful post-war economy. This is anathema to neoliberals, but allowing the market to find solutions has clearly not succeeded. It is time for a new approach.

I congratulate Prime Economics, members of the Progressive book a reality. It will provide stimulus and the opportunity for debate to all who care about our economy and wish to put an end to austerity. The next progressive government will find many policy ideas here ready for implementation.

The Progressive Economy Forum was formed in 2018 to devise a new economic programme, and brings together a council of eminent economists, many of whom have contributed essays to this book. For further information see our website: https://progressiveeconomyforum.com

# Introduction

*Jeremy Smith*

The genesis of this book is to be found in the outcome of the 2017 General Election, called by Prime Minister Theresa May with the aim of increasing her government's comfortable parliamentary majority. To the surprise of most pundits and pollsters, the final result was a government with no overall majority – and this despite, or more probably because of, the largest opposition party running on a relatively radical manifesto, and garnering 40 per cent of the popular vote.

For present purposes, we may draw two broad lessons from this outcome. First, that a large proportion of the British population no longer (if they ever did) support or accept the economic justification for austerity, nor see it as the overarching 'organising principle' for public policy. On the contrary, it was clear to them that 'austerity' was a political choice. The British Social Attitudes report for 2017, for example, found that

> After seven years of government austerity programmes by the Conservative-Liberal Democrat coalition and then Conservative majority government, the public is turning against spending less.
>
> For the first time since the financial crash of 2007-8, more people (48%) want taxation increased to allow greater spending, than want tax and spend levels to stay as they are (44%). More people (42%)

agree than disagree (28%) that government should redistribute income from the better off to those who are less well-off. Shortly before the financial crisis fewer people supported redistribution than opposed it (34% and 38% respectively in 2006). (Clery et al, 2017: 3)

This turn against the continuing policy primacy of austerity appears to have gathered strength in the post-election period. By austerity, we refer to policies that aim or claim to reduce a fiscal deficit predominantly by public spending cuts, with tax rises playing a lesser role. Indeed, in the UK a raft of tax cuts (rather than rises) accompanied spending reductions, thereby worsening inequality. The *Financial Times* commissioned the nicely named Number Cruncher Politics to undertake research, and reported on 2 May 2018:

...[P]olling we have conducted at Number Cruncher Politics reveals that an overwhelming majority of voters now feels that cuts to public services have gone too far. Asked how they felt about cuts to public spending, two in three eligible voters (66 per cent) answered "a little too far" or "much too far", with only 9 per cent thinking the cutbacks had not gone "quite far enough" or "nearly far enough ...". Austerity fatigue is strikingly broad across parties, including even a narrow majority (53 per cent) of current Conservative voters, and huge majorities of Labour voters (78 per cent) and Lib Dems (74 per cent). (Singh, 2018)

Just as importantly, the 2017 election result appeared to show that a larger number of voters were open to a wider palette of socioeconomic policies, evidenced by the breadth of support for the Labour Party's more radical manifesto programme. Proposals such as a reversal of privatisation for public utilities and the end of tuition fees for university students, for example, came back into view as electorally (as well as academically) realistic and reasonable policy choices.

This trend was surely not simply a short-term reaction to a specific political situation (post-Brexit referendum) but rather a natural reaction to longer-term trends in the economy and society. The private debt-fuelled era of liberalisation, privatisation and financial and economic deregulation, begun under the premiership of Margaret Thatcher, reaching its zenith after the fall of the Berlin Wall, but continuing to greater or lesser degrees by successive successor governments, had led inexorably to the global financial crisis of 2007–09.

For the decade thereafter, economic growth was muted and indeed the rate of growth has been falling, year on year, since 2014. Intertwined with the purely economic shifts, we have, of course, seen huge ongoing technological changes, which, in combination, have turbulent consequences for types, patterns, organisation and conditions of work. Much labour becomes more precarious, and at the foot of the social pyramid there are those who suffer the disadvantages, rather than enjoy the benefits, of our unfolding new world.

This was the backdrop to the initiative taken first by two of our editorial team (John Weeks and Jeremy Smith) who, over the summer of 2017, launched a new website under the umbrella of the Progressive Economics Group (PEG) network, which (the website stated):

> …is dedicated to the development of policy solutions based on social democratic principles to economic problems and issues. PEG policy work is publicly posted on this website, available to all political parties, organizations and individuals…. Policy briefs should address an issue or issues directly relevant to economic problems facing the United Kingdom.

The term 'social democratic principles' was not (and has not been) defined further by us; it is intended as a broad descriptor that invokes and develops a society based on a mixed economy, strong social protection, a programme to tackle inequality and discrimination, and promotion of full, good-quality employment.

The sharp-eyed reader will note that in all this there is no mention of Brexit, which (as we write this Introduction) remains an unresolved issue. This is not because we wish to downplay its importance, nor to underestimate its potential consequences for the UK's future. It is because the issues of austerity, the continued existence, scope and quality of public services, the nature and working of our social security system, the future of work and employment, all these and more are likely to be of greater direct importance to most citizens, yet have, to some degree, been ignored or relegated to the shadows of Brexit policy.

By 2018, over 30 policy briefs on a wide range of themes had been posted on the PEG site, and the idea of turning the policy proposals into book form took shape. We are very grateful to Policy Press for their support in this process. The aim of the book is however a little different from that of the website; this book will, we hope, be accessible and of interest to the active citizen who comes afresh to the issues, as well as to those already immersed in the political process and in economic debates. To that end, the original 'policy briefs' have been updated and edited, and new contributions have been added to enhance the scope of coverage, and to some degree the coherence, of the whole set.

But we emphasise that this book has grown organically from its roots as a web space open to all who wanted to contribute a proposal, and therefore it is not comprehensive in its coverage of policy issues, nor is there a silver thread of 'ideology' that shepherds the reader through the diverse contributions. It is, indeed, the diversity of contributions, allied to the genuine expertise of the contributors, that will – we hope – serve as the book's strength and guiding principle.

In the course of 'constructing' the book we had long discussions and debates about how to organise the material at our disposal, and in the end, we decided on a structure that would reflect what we see as the main pillars of social democracy, taken in the broad spirit that has inspired us.

**Part One, Building a full-employment economy**, examines the question of what might replace austerity. Rather than simply attempting to reduce government spending, the contributors consider how public money could be raised, managed and harnessed to use the full potential of the economy by creating more and better jobs and a more stable and productive economic system.

**Part Two, Public investment – Prioritising society rather than profit**, looks at how the public sector could play a positive, forward-looking and stabilising role in the development of the UK economy. Much of this is likely to be based on entirely new ways of working, including very different kinds of relationships between the state and the private sector.

**Part Three, Making finance work for society**, considers ideas about making money work for society as a means of generating wealth, and tackling problems and inequality in income and wealth distribution. These include new forms of corporate structure, new ways of banking and credit provision for smaller enterprises, as well as the roles of sovereign wealth funds and National Development Banks.

**Part Four, Genuine social security**, develops policy ideas about creating a more inclusive social security system that provides protection for all. We consider how the causes of inequality could be addressed and how the tax and benefit system, the housing market, pensions and personal finance could be reconstructed to become the basis of genuine social solidarity between individuals and generations.

**Part Five, How to provide for social needs**, looks at a number of areas that are particularly unsuited to marketisation, and considers alternative policy ideas regarding how public influence might be both extended and maintained with beneficial effects on the economy and society.

The book also includes a section on 'Jargon busters', explaining essential economic terms that are frequently – and sometimes incorrectly – used by politicians and the media. Finally, a list of 'References and further reading' is offered for those who would like to explore some of the policy ideas developed in this book.

Simply setting out this list of themes and topics demonstrates just how much unexplored or undeveloped policy terrain exists. Many of the social problems and issues that concern people most require new thinking in economic and social policy. Our book, despite the breadth of issues our contributors confront, can only touch the surface of ideas for creating a better society. But since the old mantras of austerity, reductions to public services, privatisation and deregulation – the standard fare of orthodox economic and social policy promoters since the early 1980s – are so clearly failing, it is surely time to look afresh at every area.

The aim we set at the outset for PEG was to help stimulate 'policy programmes that reflect the need for a new paradigm based on social justice, and aimed at radically regenerating and strengthening our social, economic and political system, in line with broad social democratic principles'. We offer this book in that spirit.

# Interlude: 'Mirror, mirror, on the wall – who has the highest debt of all?'

## Sue Konzelmann and Marc Fovargue-Davies

George Osborne justified his attempts to eliminate the UK's deficit, and eventually reduce debt, on the grounds that too much debt would damage the economy, increase borrowing costs and lead to a Greek-style crisis. So how much debt is too much?

The UK's figure of around 90 per cent of GDP was apparently enough to make George Osborne's eyes water – but Japan gets along quite happily with a far higher debt-to-GDP ratio of around 240 per cent of GDP.

Austerity was 'sold' to us on the false claim that a nation's accounts work like an individual, household or business budget. But since most of us can't set our own interest rates and would end up in jail if we tried printing extra money, there are some obvious problems with that argument.

A recent *Guardian* article, based on Office for National Statistics (ONS) data, gloomily concluded that 'Household debt in UK [is] "worse than any time on record"' (Inman, 2018), with British households among the most indebted of the major Western countries. The amount of debt that many of us are saddled with at the moment – around 200 per cent of household income (our equivalent to GDP) – completely destroys the argument for austerity. If a 90 per cent debt ratio is so critical – and national accounts work the same way as everyone else's – then why wasn't the government demanding that we pay it all off?

Nor is our debt the result of buying huge hi-tech TVs, new furniture and exotic holidays. Austerity makes wages go down in real terms, reduces government services, but leaves prices the same or higher – forcing people to bridge the resulting gap with credit cards or even the dreaded 'payday' loans. But there are limits – and we're reaching them. Since we can't easily create more money, adjust interest rates or revalue the currency, citizens run out of credit capacity way before the country does. So the answer to the question of debt levels is all about affordability.

But what about the ones who got us into this mess in the first place? Before the 2008 crash, they had by far the highest debt levels of all. Many banks were leveraged by around 30:1 – with some going far beyond that. That level of debt – along with equally unnerving levels of risk – did, indeed, turn out to be too high. But when the banks failed, the debt was simply transferred to the rest of us via some very questionable bailouts.

So what does all this mean? Osborne's austerity strategy was, at best, highly questionable. But there's more to it than that.

First, paying down our own and the country's debt actually means that, instead of austerity, we need successful businesses, providing both better-paying jobs and higher tax income for the government – so we need an industrial strategy that's fit for purpose. Second, since much private debt is a result of not only low wages but also high accommodation costs, we need to look for better ways of controlling those costs – through things like council homes, housing associations and rent controls. Third, we need to look long and hard at our financial sector – how it works, how much we rely on it and how we effectively regulate it.

But most of all, the policies will need to work together as a package if they are to get the job done.

# Part One: Building a full-employment economy

## Introduction

*John Weeks*

There is a general acceptance of myths about government finances and economic management that comes from a lack of understanding of public spending and taxation. Lack of understanding turns into misunderstanding under the assault of propaganda, and provides fertile soil for converting myth into accepted wisdom. Knowledge provides the mechanism to dispel these myths, to reveal accepted wisdom as myth.

Informed citizens are the foundation of democratic society. By participating through democratic institutions citizens facilitate effective government, and understanding government finances is central to that participation. In both Europe and the US few public issues are as consistently misrepresented as how governments should manage the economy, and this facilitates policies that undermine rather than enhance public welfare. To defend special interests governments can use these misrepresentations to justify policies that weaken the ability of the public to participate as citizens.

Many of us hesitate from engaging in a discussion of government budgets because of an imagined lack of expertise in what are perceived as complex subjects – because 'I am not an economist' or 'economics is too dull and difficult to try to understand'. Public sector economic management is about politics as well as economics, yet many politicians and much of the media discuss government economic policies as if constrained by economic imperatives. Those imperatives themselves are frequently treated as natural forces beyond the control of governments and citizens. Debates over political priorities are too frequently treated as if they were a technical matter for an expert elite.

This first part of this book takes the reader past surface rhetoric for a straightforward discussion of government economic management, 'fiscal policy' (public spending, taxation and the balance between the two), monetary policy and the Bank of England, and the functional role of public deficits and the public debt. Understanding the nine 'policy ideas' in this part of the book requires no prior knowledge of economics, only an inquiring and open mind.

The ideas that follow all challenge the prevailing orthodoxy on economic management and the role of the public sector. Mainstream ideology on economic management preaches that the main task of policy-makers is to balance the public budget and keep inflation low. That combination will allegedly stabilise the overall economy, automatically ensuring full utilisation of resources and employment for all. All nine of the topics in this initial part challenge that approach to economic management, revealing its flaws and proposing an alternative framework.

As with the other parts of this book, this one lays out a framework for an equitable economic system that provides work for all who seek it, with decent pay and conditions. Central to that framework is protection against the instability inherent in markets that manifest themselves in boom and bust. Overall economic stability, 'macroeconomic stability', represents a necessary condition for such a system.

Sue Konzelmann's presentation of the alternative approach begins by addressing the ideology of austerity, showing its limited relevance and applicability. The critique of austerity implies the need to develop an alternative progressive approach. Reinforcing that critique, John Weeks inspects fiscal policy and the role of the public budget in implementing the alternative to austerity. And no serious analysis of the overall economic framework is possible without addressing the gender impact of macroeconomic policy, which is the focus of the contribution by Susan Himmelweit and Mary-Ann Stephenson.

John Weeks follows the gender analysis by confronting the ideology of price stability through low inflation. Jan Toporowski complements the critique of price stability by arguing that the focus of Bank of England policy should not be inflation management. If that task becomes secondary, a new mandate is required, which he proposes with an innovative focus. These aspects of monetary policy naturally lead to an issue central to the austerity ideology, the public debt. John Weeks dispels the considerable mystification and obfuscation about public debt, showing it functions as an asset as well as a liability.

The confusions and obfuscations about the role of taxation in a market economy match those plaguing discussion of public debt. Rarely in the media do we find serious analytical discussion of the social function of taxation. Oliver Wendell Holmes, famous US Supreme Court Justice, wrote in a 1927 decision 'taxes are what we pay for civilized society'. Very much in that vein, John Weeks discusses the role of progressive taxation, followed by Richard Murphy's proposal for a new Ministry of Tax.

Part One finishes with Jeremy Smith addressing an issue heavily laden with ideology – whether our government should be constrained in its spending policies, whether it should operate within 'fiscal rules'. This issue involves aspects of economic theory and analysis, as well the politics of policy-making.

## Policy ideas

1. When is austerity an *appropriate* economic policy? *Sue Konzelmann*
2. Using the budget to manage output and employment *John Weeks*
3. Why assessing the equality impact of economic policies matters *Susan Himmelweit and Mary-Ann Stephenson*
4. How should we manage inflation? *John Weeks*
5. What should guide monetary policy? *Jan Toporowski*
6. Does the UK really have too much debt? *John Weeks*

# POLICY IDEA 1

## When is austerity an *appropriate* economic policy?

*Sue Konzelmann*

**What's the issue?**

The results of the consistent application of austerity policies – cuts in public expenditure and/or increased taxation – since the Conservative-led coalition government came to power in 2010 do not make for encouraging reading. Although politicians have claimed that austerity means 'living within our means', the reality for the vast majority of British citizens is very different.

Not only have critical public services been either withdrawn or severely limited by the progressive removal of social protections, both GDP and wage growth have also been constrained. Austerity has also failed to deliver its stated objectives – of rapidly reducing and then eliminating the government's deficit (the difference between its annual expenditures and revenues) and national debt (the accumulation of any previous deficits and interest charges plus the current year's deficit).

But the fundamental question isn't whether austerity is a 'good' or 'bad' policy. Rather, it is whether austerity is an *appropriate* policy, given a particular economic situation.

## When is austerity an *appropriate* economic policy?

## Analysis

Eight years after the turn to austerity in 2010, the UK's recovery from the recession, precipitated by the 2008 financial crisis, is its slowest in recorded history. The government's initial response was to rescue financial institutions deemed 'too big to fail' and engage in emergency fiscal and monetary stimulus, and by 2010, a weak recovery was underway, with GDP returning to growth of 1.7 per cent. But concerns about rising government deficits (which increased from 2.6 per cent of GDP in 2007 to 10.1 per cent in 2009) and high levels of public debt (which, during the same period, had risen from 41.9 to 64.1 per cent of GDP) caused an *apparent* sharp reversal in policy. 'Apparent' because, although the word hadn't yet been popularised, austerity has been the policy of all Tory governments since 1979.

The Greek sovereign debt crisis served as the catalyst for austerity in the European Union (EU). In the UK, although the government's deficits and public debt were a direct result of the bank bailouts and emergency stimulus measures, the crisis was redefined as a 'crisis of debt'; it was (falsely) alleged that high levels of public deficits and debt were the result of excessive government spending. From this perspective, investors – that is, speculators – in government bonds were assumed to be worried about the increased risk of sovereign debt default. So unless government deficits and public debt were reduced, bond yields – the cost of government debt – would rise sharply, adding to the cost of borrowing, and hence to the public deficit and accumulated national debt.

The idea that public deficits and debt have a negative effect on investor confidence is rooted in the belief that a state's creditworthiness rests upon a balanced budget: fiscal deficits and public debt are held to erode confidence in the government's ability to repay those debts. By contrast, austerity is seen to have a positive effect on confidence – not only of government bond holders but also of consumers and businesses – and hence on private sector spending.

However, unlike Greece, for which (as a member of the Eurozone) the risk of sovereign debt default is a credible one, the UK is in no risk of default. This is because it both borrows in its own currency and has a flexible exchange rate. So, if necessary, it has the ability to print money and devalue its currency to manage its debt. In addition, the Bank of England can prevent a rise in interest rates by purchasing public bonds at a fixed rate.

To persuade voters that austerity was indeed required, a number of other arguments have been made. Perhaps the most common one has been the likening of the government's budget to that of a household or business, which requires balancing. This analogy dates back centuries, to the time when government budgets were mainly spent on wars and national emergencies – and there was no such thing as either permanent spending on social welfare or revenues from income tax. However, once the government came to rely heavily on income taxes for its revenue, and with the expansion of social welfare commitments during the first part of the 20th century – both of which have a dampening effect on growth during recessions – the logic supporting this argument disappeared.

A less common argument is that first made by John Maynard Keynes during the 1920s and 1930s. Keynes also saw an essential role for austerity – but as a necessary counterpart to stimulus, to be applied during the boom, when the economy's resources are fully employed, as a means of cooling an overheating economy and thereby averting inflation or financial collapse. This makes the use of stimulus sustainable, by liquidating the cyclical deficit – the part of the deficit caused by fluctuations in government spending and revenues resulting from the economic cycle – and providing the funds to deal with future recessions.

Despite the questionable nature of the arguments in support of austerity when the economy is in recession, the *politics* of austerity trumped the economics, and in 2009 the term 'age of austerity' – which had earlier been used to describe the years immediately following the First World War – was popularised by the Conservative Party leader, David Cameron, who declared that 'the age of irresponsibility is giving way to the age of austerity' (Cameron, 2009), pledging to put an end to excessive government spending if elected in the following year's general election.

The 2010 General Election produced a Conservative-led coalition government, and in his first budget speech, the new Chancellor, George Osborne, told the House of Commons that 'unless we deal with our debts, there will be no growth' (Osborne, 2010). He then announced a £40 billion 'emergency' austerity budget that included significant tax increases (including VAT) and cuts in social welfare and other areas of public expenditure, with the objective of eliminating the full employment deficit – the part of the deficit that remains even after growth has returned to normal – and reducing public debt by the end of Parliament in 2015.

But rather than hastening the recovery, austerity slowed it, and the promised private sector-led expansion failed to materialise. Between 2010 and 2012, GDP growth stagnated, at rates well below 2 per cent; unemployment remained stubbornly high, at around 8 per cent, compared with pre-crisis rates of about 5 per cent; and, due to continued public deficits, government debt continued to rise, reaching 84.5 per cent of GDP in 2012.

Later that year, the government's austerity programme – which had, in practice, involved a sharp reduction in the *rate of increase* in public expenditure (as opposed to an absolute reduction) and large absolute cuts to local government grants (which do not appear in the central government budget) – was quietly relaxed. However, the political rhetoric continued, and by 2013, all three main parties endorsed deficit reductions as the central component of the government's fiscal policy.

But by the end of Parliament, the coalition government's record on the economy had not lived up to its promises. Economic growth had been significantly reduced, averaging 2 per cent per year, compared with 2.6 per cent for the period 1948 to 2007. Slower growth meant lower tax revenues and increased social welfare costs, despite tax increases and public spending cuts.

Thus, although the government's deficit as a percentage of GDP had been reduced to 4.3 per cent, less than half of its level in 2010, it was still higher than the coalition had predicted, and, although the sale of government assets (mostly shares of stock in the nationalised banks) had slowed the rate of increase in public debt, which stood at 88.2 per cent of GDP in 2015, it was 17 per cent higher than it had been when the coalition came to power, and it was continuing to rise as a consequence of the failure to turn the government's deficit into surplus.

By 2018, despite austerity's failure to achieve its stated objectives in relation to the government's deficits and debt (which, at the end of 2017, stood at 1.9 and 87.7 per cent of GDP, respectively) – let alone its damaging impact on the vast majority of UK citizens, particularly those most reliant on public services – the government was persisting with its programme of austerity.

## What can we do?

Booms and recessions have been a fact of life for at least the past two centuries, and during much of that time, urgent calls for reducing public debt have accompanied recessions – when government deficits and public debt naturally increase – rather than booms, when this dynamic is reversed. However, counter-intuitive though it might seem, this is exactly the wrong way round.

From an *economic* perspective, the choice between austerity and stimulus depends entirely on the state of the economy rather than the state of public finances. The following policy ideas for austerity policy would serve the interests of the many:

- **Austerity is an *appropriate* policy during a boom, when the economic risk is overheating, inflation and financial crisis.** In this context, discretionary increases in taxes and/or reductions in public expenditure will have the effect of cooling the economy and averting inflation and the risk of financial crisis. They will also tend to eliminate the deficits and generate a surplus, providing the budgetary resources to deal with future recessions.
- **Austerity is an *inappropriate* policy during a recession.** In this context, increasing taxes and/or reducing public expenditure, when the economy is already weak, will only serve to deepen and lengthen the slump. It will also worsen

rather than improve the government's deficit and add to public debt, because the slower economic growth that austerity causes results in slower increases in government revenue. It is simple arithmetic: revenue stagnates because GDP stagnates, which increases the budget deficit and the public debt, causing both the public deficit to GDP ratio (deficit/GDP) and the public debt to GDP ratio (debt/GDP) to rise.

# POLICY IDEA 2

# Using the budget to manage output and employment

## John Weeks

## What's the issue?

After the UK economy showed recovery in 2009 and early 2010, eight years of austerity policies by Conservative governments brought recession, stagnation and faltering growth. Various excuses offered by Tory politicians, from world market instability to Brexit anxieties, fail to conceal the basic cause of this historically dismal economic performance. In the foreseeable future it will be the responsibility of a different government to manage rationally the economy.

> What policy framework will a future government use to maintain a high and stable level of employment and output?

## Analysis

Much of the public and many politicians believe that commitment to match public revenue with public expenditure represents a sensible, sound and achievable fiscal policy. This generally accepted fiscal balance rule (FBR) gives rise to several sources of disagreement: (1) when and how rapidly to achieve it; (2) what specific measure of the budget requires balancing; and (3) what policies the government should apply to bring the balance about.

This deficit obsession of Tory governments makes all public expenditure policy captive to hitting the zero overall fiscal balance, or overshoot into surplus. Until recently the repeated failures to achieve fiscal targets did not weaken the grip of this extreme version of the FBR over the public mind and the media.

Even the Institute for Fiscal Studies focuses on the minutiae of the fiscal deficit rather than critiquing the ideology of the budget balancing. Even worse, Tory chancellors suffer criticism for not eliminating borrowing, although doing so would provoke recession. The responsible approach to this fiscal mismanagement is not to bicker over the likely success of reaching a balanced public budget, but to label the policy for what it is – pernicious nonsense.

Tory success in inculcating belief in the virtue of balanced budgets has proved so ideologically successful that it compels all politicians to commit to some balancing rule. By contrast, the Labour Shadow Chancellor, John McDonnell, proposed a flexible and non-ideological variation. The McDonnell budget guideline commits the Treasury to balancing current (that is, non-capital investment) expenditure and revenue as a targeted outcome of policies to maintain a high level of employment and output, not as a goal that overrides all other policies.

A basic problem with the FBR in all its versions is the inherent improbability of achieving it. The improbability emerges clearly when we inspect the conditions for its successful implementation. Private and public demand together determine the level of national income, which, since 2010, has stagnated below its potential. To keep the discussion simple, I leave out foreign trade, treat private investment as constant and public revenue as strictly proportional to national income (for example, at 35 per cent), and assume current household disposable income determines current household consumption.

We start with a negative budget balance in the context of a Conservative government. The Tory Chancellor is committed to reducing the deficit quickly, and can increase taxes or reduce expenditure. Conservative Chancellors have favoured expenditure cuts. Expenditure cuts reduce aggregate demand, that is, they reduce expenditure on goods and services produced in the economy. Lower production causes a fall in those employed to generate that production, with the result national income. These declines result in a fall in corporate and household tax payments. As a result, public borrowing declines by less than the cuts themselves, because the cuts lead to declines in incomes and public revenue.

In this simple case, in order to maintain orderly fiscal management and meet specified targets the Chancellor must have an accurate estimate of an interactive system that includes the effect of a cut in public expenditure on tax revenue. To assess this interaction the Chancellor and advisers need to know at the minimum the values of two key behavioural relationships: (1) how much more tax people and corporations pay when incomes change, and, closely related, (2) how much their spending changes when their incomes change.

The repeated failures of Tory governments to meet their own fiscal targets demonstrate that the concrete, real-world feedbacks, determined by these two relationships, prove extremely difficult to estimate. Complications include the openness of the UK economy to foreign trade (spending on imports or domestic goods and services), variations in time of adjustment for revenue collection, and private investment decisions. Estimates of macroeconomic interactions can be made, but they come with a substantial marginal of error ('random variation'). When to the feedback interactions we add changes in tax rates and regulations, forecasts become uncertain to the point of unpredictable.

Eventually expenditure reductions will balance the public budget, albeit at the cost of recession. Far more complicated than chasing a zero deficit is to balance expenditure and revenue in an economy with changing levels of output, 'over the business cycle'. Calculating the interactions and feedbacks among economic variables over time when basic parameters such as tax rates change is the most obvious problem with a multi-year fiscal commitment.

Even prior to that, intractability begins with defining and measuring 'the economic cycle', which, in practice, can only be done after it ends. However, an over-the-cycle fiscal target requires a before-the-event (*ex ante*) estimate of the future course of the economy. Neither the beginning nor the end of a cycle is predictable, even in principle.

Because a promise to 'balance the books' is retrospective, achieving it depends on definition and measurement. One cycle ends when the next begins. That tautology provides no guide to policy. Definition and measurement of cycles should not be tasks assigned either to the Treasury or the Office for Budget Responsibility (OBR). The Treasury has a conflict of interest because it never wants to be wrong. The OBR is unlikely to have competence in economic forecasting beyond the immediate future, and economic cycles typically last several years.

More fundamental than definition and measurement is what a Chancellor thinks causes 'the economic cycle'. The Cameron and May governments viewed the cycle as a natural phenomenon that occurs independently of the actions of policy-makers. It cannot be avoided. Like the weather, the government can only prepare for its impact ('repair the roof while the sun shines', Osborne was fond of saying).

Managing the economic cycle to minimise instability requires management of revenue and expenditure. Expenditure policies are a major determinant of tax revenue flows. For an enlightened Chancellor the expenditure–revenue interaction is a blessing because of the automatic stabilising effect of revenue flows. The balance between revenue and expenditure, 'making ends meet', becomes an outcome derivative from the primary task of a rational, pragmatic Chancellor, minimising market instability for the economy as a whole.

This rational approach to fiscal management, in contrast to the illusion of deficit management, can, under unusual circumstances, encounter a public debt constraint. Since the end of the Second World War this constraint has not been operative for UK policy-makers. Understanding the nature of this constraint and why it is unlikely requires overcoming an ideological phobia as powerful as an obsession with balancing budgets (see Policy idea 7, later in this part of the book).

## What can we do?

Rational economic policy involves using capital expenditure to stimulate medium and long-term growth and current expenditure to keep the economy at a stable and high level of output and employment. The policy ideas for this active fiscal policy are as follows:

- **Public investment (the capital budget)** is the instrument to stimulate growth. Because many capital investments require extended construction periods, public investment is relatively inflexible in the short run. This inflexibility makes it an inefficient instrument for management of output and employment.
- **Current expenditure** provides the tool to counteract the waxing and waning of private investment and exports that would otherwise cause overheating and underutilisation.
- **The public budget may show a surplus or a deficit** during this regime of active fiscal policy depending on the budget measure selected, the time period and private sector behaviour. Vigorous private sector demand favours a fiscal surplus, and weak private spending implies a fiscal deficit. By dampening cyclical extremes, demand management indirectly moderates variations in revenue flow.
- **The balance between expenditure and taxation** is the outcome of an active fiscal policy, not a policy goal.

# POLICY IDEA 3

# Why assessing the equality impact of economic policies matters

*Susan Himmelweit and Mary-Ann Stephenson*

**What's the issue?**

The public sector equality duty (PSED), contained in the Equality Act 2010, requires public bodies to have 'due regard to the need to eliminate discrimination, advance equality of opportunity and foster good relations between different people' when carrying out their activities. This applies to all 'protected characteristics', such as race, sex, disability, age, sexual orientation, and to policy-making at all levels – central, national and local.

The PSED has had a positive impact on equality practice within public authorities and, to a limited extent, in policy-making. However, its aim was to bring about a transformative approach to equality by going beyond simply outlawing discrimination to tackle inequality at a structural level. The duty has failed to fulfil this aim.

In particular, there has been a failure to consider the gender equality impact of a number of economic policies. This is true not only of the government, but also of the manifesto commitments of opposition parties (with the exception of the Women's Equality Party).

## Why does knowing about the gender impact of policies make for better policy-making?

### Analysis

The Equality Act 2010, which included the PSED, was one of the last Acts passed under the Labour government. Practice in implementing it has therefore been set by the coalition and subsequent Conservative governments.

The coalition government made a number of changes to the duty that reduced both its scope and its effectiveness. These included the removal of the socioeconomic duty, which would have required policy-makers to consider the impact of their policies on income-based inequality as well as other forms of inequality.

The government has also weakened the PSED in its implementation. It has significantly cut the budget and remit of the Equality and Human Rights Commission (EHRC), the body responsible for monitoring and enforcement of the PSED. Ministers have questioned the need for public bodies to carry out equality impact assessments (EIAs) and government departments have failed to publish them, making it impossible to judge whether 'due regard' has been paid to equality considerations.

In terms of economic policy, the government claims that the PSED applies to the spending of individual government departments, such as health, education and so on, and to that of local authorities, but that it does not apply to the allocation of funds by the Treasury to those other public bodies. It does not see the PSED as requiring that due regard be paid, for example, to the impact on the gender employment gap of allocating funds to defence rather than local authorities. This is even though cuts to the latter have been largely responsible for the greater employment impact of austerity on women, through the loss of public sector jobs, reduction in services and consequent increased needs for unpaid family care, while defence spending impacts mainly on men's employment.

The Treasury does, however, recognise that individual tax measures are its responsibility and so, on each measure it, or rather HM Revenue & Customs (HMRC), publishes its EIA. There are of very variable quality. In the past, the gender equality impact of not raising fuel tax was dismissed with the argument that men and women who drive similar cars and for similar distances will be similarly impacted by a rise in fuel tax. This woefully misunderstands the meaning of an EIA. An EIA requires examining existing inequalities (in car ownership/miles driven etc) and seeing if policies reduce or increase them, and if the latter, considering mitigating measures to counteract those adverse effects.

By now, HMRC does seem to understand that for individual measures, but it still does not produce any statement about the cumulative gender (or any other) EIA of all its measures. It's through such cumulative analysis that we can see where austerity has impacted most severely, for the Women's Budget Group has shown that between 2010 and 2020 the combined effect of tax and benefit changes and public spending cuts has resulted in the poorest Black and Asian households experiencing the biggest drop in living standard, of 19.2 per cent and 20.1 per cent respectively, compared with a loss of between 4 per cent and 5 per cent for the wealthiest households.

It is not only the government that has failed to take assessing equality impact seriously. The Labour Party's 2017 election manifesto promised that 'A Labour government will gender audit all policy and legislation for its impact on women before implementation' (Labour Party 'A More Equal Society' manifesto). This is very promising. However, for that to be effective, it must be carried out consistently before policies are decided upon and on all policy, not only those where such a gender impact is to be expected.

Indeed, it is the overarching macroeconomic policies that tend to have the greatest gender impact, often greater than that of policies directly designed to rectify inequalities. That same manifesto also cites with approval Labour's fiscal credibility rule that 'Labour will borrow only to invest', but nowhere is it stated what is meant by 'investment'. As 'Investing in social infrastructure' (Part Two, Policy idea 6, this volume) argues, a concept of investment that counts only spending that creates physical infrastructure (to build bridges, roads etc) and not spending that creates social infrastructure (on education, health and care services) is biased against women, increasing several gender inequalities, including the gender employment gap. Quite apart from any other criticisms of it, a fiscal credibility rule that allows borrowing to invest but does not include investment in social infrastructure has clearly not been assessed for the gender equality impact. If it had been, either it would have been amended to clarify that it includes social investment, or additional measures would have been proposed to mitigate its adverse gender equality impacts.

Another example is the promise made not to raise income tax for those earning below £80,000 a year, while allocating just £4 billion to rectifying the cuts to social security benefits since 2010. The promise not to raise income tax (the fairest tax that we have) for 95 per cent of taxpayers does nothing for the poorest in society. The 43 per cent of adults who earn too little to pay income tax, 66 per cent of whom are women, gain nothing from it. They will also gain nothing from £24 billion a year given away in tax cuts through raising tax thresholds since 2010. Over the same period, over £12 billion of cuts in spending on social security have hit women far harder than men. By proposing to replace only a third of this, while keeping Tory give-aways to income tax payers, Labour is bringing in a combination of policies that will inevitably increase gender inequalities in income. The tax and social security systems need to be reformed together. Making promises not to raise tax for large numbers of income tax payers, while not promising to replace cuts made to the income of those relying on benefits, just entrenches gender inequalities.

Labour may argue that raising the minimum wage will benefit women and reduce the need for social security spending, but there was nothing in its manifesto to show that it had worked out whether the impact overall would be positive or negative on gender equality. A proper gender equality impact analysis of these polices would have shown this up.

## What can we do?

- **Policy-makers need to show greater commitment to ensuring that the gender, and other equality, impacts of its policies are taken into account in policy formation.** The socioeconomic duty of the PSED should be restored.
- Further, government and opposition parties need to invest in improving their own understanding and capacity to analyse the equality impact of policies across a range of inequalities and number of dimensions of inequality. To do so, and to keep up-to-date with developing equality issues, **policy-makers should consult with civil society organisations skilled in analysing equality impacts, drawing on their expertise at an early stage in policy-making**.
- **It is important that the public and media are also engaged in monitoring the equality impact of policies.** This requires that policy-makers carry out and *publish* high-quality EIAs of the full range of social and economic policies, including their cumulative impact. Where policies are shown to have an adverse equality impact, either they should be abandoned or other mitigating measures should be proposed and implemented to counteract that adverse effect.
- **A consistent commitment to reducing inequalities is needed throughout policy-making**, including in the formation of macroeconomic policy. This includes scrutinising the traditional categories of economic thinking for inherent biases. In particular, the meaning of 'investment' needs to be redefined to include social investment, and tax and social security policy need to be analysed and reviewed together, if we are to have a more progressive system that reduces rather than entrenches existing inequalities.

# POLICY IDEA 4

# How should we manage inflation?

*John Weeks*

### What's the issue?

For four decades British governments have placed priority on maintaining low inflation. Under Conservative governments this functioned as a central macroeconomic policy goal. A progressive government will come under strong pressure to maintain this priority, although it is frequently in conflict with other objectives such as economic growth and full employment.

> What is the appropriate inflation guideline for a progressive government?

### Analysis

Private sector price increases are simultaneously increases in private sector incomes:

[price = intermediate costs + value added], [value added = wages + profits + other incomes]

By definition price increases do not themselves erode real wages. Real wages and more generally household real incomes fall as a result of the distributional effects of price increases on incomes (wages and profits) and expenditures (spending patterns across the income distribution). When private sector prices go up, private incomes go up by the same proportion. However, some incomes go up by more than other incomes. Distribution, and not the inflation rate, is the key issue.

The standard definition of inflation is 'a general and continuous increase in prices implying a fall in the purchasing power of money'. Several empirical yardsticks exist to assess the degree of inflation, prices paid by households on final goods and services ('consumer' price indices, CPI), prices paid by producers, wholesale indices and aggregate output (GDP) deflators. Each of these measures can serve a different purpose. All have the same failing of treating an increase in the index as indicating inflation.

'A general increase in prices' need not imply 'a fall in the purchasing power of money'. A price increase may indicate an improvement in the quality of a good or service. For example, from 2000 to 2016 in Britain the price of new motor vehicles rose by 20 per cent. Part of this increase represented quality change, not inflation. A closely related source of non-inflationary price increase is the introduction of new products, such as computer-regulated fuel injection in motor vehicles.

A 1995 study for the US Congress, the Boskin Report, concluded that quality change and new products accounted for 1.1 to 1.3 percentage points in the CPI (Boskin, 1996). Less detailed work by the Bank of England and the European Central Bank reached the same conclusion, that an increase in composite price indices does not necessarily imply general price inflation (although there is no consensus on the degree of overestimation).

Every index includes many prices and their average increase is a statistical outcome affected by method of calculation. Measurement as well as definition means inflation is a 'general rise in prices'. The phrase abstracts from the different ways in which prices are determined. Except in rare circumstances, all prices do not rise, and, if they do, it is not in the same proportion across goods and services. The heterogeneous behaviour of prices should guide policy-makers, not the changes in the composite index.

All goods and services fall into one of two categories – those whose price is strongly influenced by international trade and those determined primarily in UK domestic exchange. Following international guidelines for assigning goods and services to each category, detailed price data from the Office for National Statistics (ONS) indicate that 56 per cent of consumer expenditure goes to international goods and services and 44 per cent on domestic goods and services. The former category contains most of the goods covered by the index; the latter is overwhelmingly services.

These two categories of goods and services behaved quite differently over the 21 years, 1997–2017, as Figure 1 shows. During 2008–12 the two take a similar pattern, but for most years the correspondence is weak. For the entire period the annualised rate of change of domestic prices was more than double the rate for the international category (3.0 per cent and 1.4 per cent, respectively, and 1.9 per cent for the CPI as a whole). Prices of domestic goods and services were more stable, reflecting the volatility of primary products in international markets, most obviously petroleum.

The distinction between international and domestic goods and services in the measures of inflation used by UK policy-makers has major policy importance, and should guide the inflation policy for a progressive government. This is because:

- The potential for the British government and the Bank of England to influence the prices of international goods and services is limited.
- The domestic category consists overwhelmingly of services, public sector services (14 per cent of the CPI) and private sector services (30 per cent).
- With few exceptions, the prices of public sector services are not determined through markets.
- Trade unions are weak or absent in private sector services, and the sector has the highest incidence of poverty of any in the economy (for example, domestic service).

**Figure 1:** Annualised rate of monthly price changes for domestic and international goods and services, CPI, June 1997–June 2017

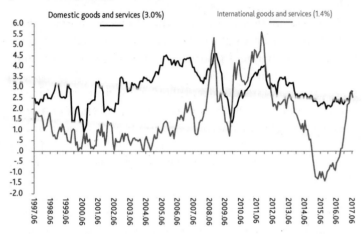

In practice, anti-inflationary monetary policies achieve their purpose largely through restraining the growth of wages in private services. Private sector services account for about 30 per cent of the CPI, and, for the economy as a whole, the share of wages in national income is about 55 per cent. If this share applies to private services it implies that a one percentage point fall in the overall CPI would require a 6 per cent fall for wages in private services.

## What can we do?

A general and continuous increase in prices is simultaneously a general and continuous increase in incomes, and cannot in itself reduce purchasing power. This implies that a policy of low inflation will not protect the purchasing power of the working class or that of households in the lower income groups.

Mainstream anti–inflation policies such as raising interest rates work through demand reduction. This approach tends to undermine the incomes of the non-rich. The following guidelines for price stability would serve the interests of the majority of the population:

- **End Bank of England inflation targets** so that these no longer function as a policy constraint. Inflation targeting places the burden of price stability on the working class and especially low-paid workers in private services.

- **Abandon composite price indices as guides to price stability.** These are misleading and carry a deflationary bias.
- **Correctly define inflation** (better incorporating quality effects).
- **Make price stability policy derivative from overall macroeconomic management** (objectives for employment, economic growth and external balance).

The formal statement of government policy might therefore be:

> The government seeks to maintain a high level of employment with rising incomes accompanied by a degree of price stability consistent with financial stability and sustainable external balances.

# POLICY IDEA 5

# What should guide monetary policy?

*Jan Toporowski*

## What's the issue?

Two decades after the granting of independence to the Bank of England to determine its own monetary policy, the doctrine that formed the basis for this policy has been discredited by the financial crisis of 2007–10 and its aftermath. This doctrine was the 'New Consensus on Monetary Policy', the view that monetary policy should function by varying the interest rate at which the central bank provides funds to the money market. The New Consensus presumed that setting the central bank rate would effectively regulate the rate of inflation and the business cycle.

With quantitative easing discredited, what principles should guide the practice of UK monetary policy?

## Analysis

After the global financial crisis at the end of the 2000s, inflation slumped despite the so-called extraordinary measure of quantitative easing (QE). Exchange rate shocks following the European Union (EU) referendum and internationally transferred price increases have determined UK inflation rates. Associated with price behaviour are increasing concerns about 'secular stagnation' and the effect on the financial stability of the central bank of purchases of long-term securities from private corporations (so-called QE). The blame for the failure of the 1990s New Consensus policy doctrine has been placed on the monetary transmission mechanism from the cutting of central bank interest rates to private lending. The absence of any economic rebound after interest rates was attributed to the 'breakdown' of this mechanism. No alternative doctrine or theory has emerged to guide central bank operations.

The monetary transmission mechanism is not a mechanical process. It does not 'break down', but alters with the changing structure of the financial markets. A structural examination of the financial markets rather than an examination of financial indicators shows why QE policy ceased to work. Development of dollar swap markets internationalised UK money markets. With the exception of the US Federal Reserve System, no central bank in a country without capital controls can use money markets as the starting point of a transmission mechanism of that central bank's monetary policy. Cross-border capital movements overwhelm Bank of England actions.

Monetary policy, as shown by QE, operates on capital markets for long-term securities rather than on short-term money markets and the real economy. Systematic flaws in capital markets turned the financial crash of 2008 into a financially induced depression. Large industrial corporations were unable to refinance short-term debts into long-term bonds and equity. They responded to this illiquidity in capital markets by cutting back their investment in fixed capital.

Growing awareness of the threats to financial stability of QE has not led to a development of a sound alternative. Instead, the question of how QE could be discontinued so dominated consensus monetary policy discussions. However, a return to the *status quo ante* would be the wrong policy approach. Abandoning QE would leave the capital markets short of liquidity, creating problems for government budgets and corporate finance, both of which need to be facilitated in order to overcome the slow economic growth.

## What can we do?

- **The new policy framework should regulate liquidity in the capital markets** by building on QE open market operations. Capital market liquidity is needed to support bond markets, including the government bond market, and to regulate corporate liquidity. Regulating capital market liquidity requires reinforcement through taxing holdings of financial assets to discourage hoarding of liquidity. The framework aims to drain off the liquidity created by government deficit spending.
- **Taxation of holdings of financial assets and drawing off excess liquidity implies that monetary policy must coordinate with fiscal policy.** This need not alter the independence of the central bank, nor subordinate the monetary policy of the Bank of England to government guidance. Fiscal policy coordination could be achieved by making the Bank of England more accountable to Parliament for financial stability in capital markets. Parliament would assign the Bank of England responsibility for ensuring adequate liquidity in capital markets. This could be measured by stock market indices and the ease of issue of new securities by the government and by corporations based in England.
- **The Bank of England could regulate the liquidity in a globalised capital market** by setting as its target a stable yield curve – interest rate by duration of the bond – for UK government bonds and for liabilities of British corporations that are willing to have markets for their long-term securities regulated by the Bank. This would also give the Bank control over those corporations' merger and acquisition activities. This policy framework was used informally in the 19th century, when capital markets were internationalised under the gold

standard. Central banks then made a market in bonds issued by their governments and had formal and informal lists of corporate securities that they would accept for purchase.

- **The framework would provide a tool to implement the industrial policy found in the Labour manifesto.** In return for benefiting from the Bank of England's liquidity provision, UK corporations could be expected to show a greater commitment to investment in Britain. The stabilisation of the yield curve and the regulation of merger and takeover activity would also discourage speculation and trading on capital market instability.

- **The stabilisation of the capital market would complement and make more effective bank capital adequacy regimes.** Banks lending to businesses with access to more stable long-term funding would improve the stability of their outstanding loans.

# POLICY IDEA 6

# Does the UK really have too much debt?

*John Weeks*

**What's the issue?**

During 2008–11 the Labour government successfully implemented counter-cyclical fiscal policy to moderate the impact of the global financial crisis. As a result of the fiscal deficits in those years, the outstanding net public debt by the generally accepted measure rose from £560 billion in mid-2007 to £1.1 trillion by the 2010 General Election. Despite the austerity rhetoric of the subsequent coalition and Conservative governments, by mid-2018 the debt reached £1.7 trillion.

Is the present level of debt a problem requiring action? Need the debt be reduced, and is it a burden on current or future generations?

## Analysis

The UK government has the tools to prevent debt default and excessive interest rates. These are not and will not be problems. Britain has a national currency managed by a national central bank. As a result, the British government can never default. It can replace maturing public bonds with new ones. Should private buyers refuse to purchase the bonds at the interest rate set by the British government, those bonds can be sold to the Bank of England. The option to sell to the Bank of England provides a mechanism to prevent excessively high bond rates.

**The size of the public debt is not a problem.** Figure 2 shows that publicly issued bonds or 'gilts' amounted to just over £2 trillion, which was 96 per cent of GDP at mid-2018. This standard measure used by the Treasury is in line with international practice. It equals total public bonds minus government liquid assets such as Treasury holdings of foreign currencies. Part of that amount, £251 billion, represented government ownership of nationalised banks, the largest public holding in HSBC. While technically a liability, these bonds have an equivalent asset in bank balance sheets, bringing the effective debt down to 84 per cent of GDP.

The Bank of England held about 23 per cent of this amount (£466 billion), most of it the result of asset purchases from private corporations, so-called quantitative easing (QE). When this amount of debt, what the public sector owed itself, is subtracted, we get the *outstanding debt*, the debt that the UK government owes to others. The outstanding debt falls to 62 per cent of GDP, far below the typically cited statistic. In 2018 the outstanding public debt was not almost equal to national production (GDP), as frequently asserted.

**The public debt is not a burden.** Along with confusion about the size of the debt goes misunderstanding of the nature of the UK debt, especially with regard to ownership.

The public sector itself owns 23 per cent of the £2 trillion UK gross public debt (see Figure 3). The government pays the interest on this portion of the debt to itself. Thus, almost a quarter of the debt and the interest paid on it are not a burden. Pension funds hold a large portion of the 75 per cent of gilts not owned

**Figure 2:** UK public debt as a percentage of GDP (end of 2016)

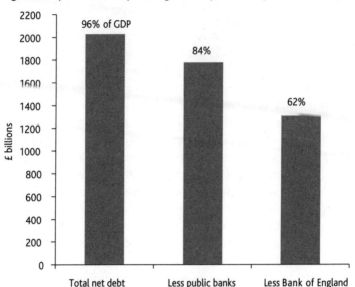

by the government. The interest paid on debt held by pension funds is income to households. This is a source of household income, a benefit, not a burden. The distributional effect of these interest payments is likely to be negative, because most households with private pensions have above-average incomes. A more progressive tax system would reduce this inequality effect. It is not in itself an effect of the public debt.

Debt held by the government itself and pension funds are long-term holdings, rarely marketed. When these are subtracted, the remaining gilts compose the market-active public debt, which is slightly less than half the total. Only the £548 billion of gilts held by foreign creditors could be considered a 'burden', in that the associated interest payments are from UK taxpayers to non-UK creditors. For the fiscal year 2017/18 interest payments to foreign creditors were slightly less than £15 billion, implying quite a small debt burden of 0.7 per cent of GDP.

In addition, consideration of the burden of the debt must include analysis of its role in monetary policy and financial stability. Local governments, financial institutions and non-financial corporations all accumulate cash from sale of assets or

**Figure 3:** Public debt ownership at the end of 2016

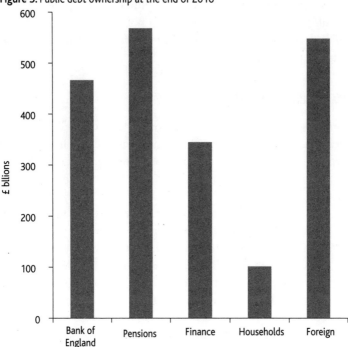

profits. Government bonds provide the safest form in which to protect the value of these holdings. The substantial corporate demand for public bonds as store of value appears to have created a shortage at the end of the 2010s. Public provision of a safe store of value provides an important risk-reducing and stabilising function for the private sector.

Public bonds also serve as an instrument of monetary policy. When the Treasury or the Bank of England considers that the private sector suffers from a shortage of liquidity ('cash'), the purchase of public bonds provides one method of solution; for example, the purchase of £10 billion worth of public bonds from commercial banks increases bank reserves in the hope that increased bank lending will result. When inflationary pressures appear, the sale of public bonds reduces bank liquidity.

Recognition of the role public bonds play in the private economy should make it clear that, while public debt can, under some circumstances, be excessive, public debt can also be too small. Polemical calls to pay off the public debt indicate a lack of understanding of the important functions of public bonds in a market economy.

## What can we do?

Analysis of the nature, size and ownership of the UK public debt shows that it poses no threat to economic stability, its size is modest, it helps stabilise the private economy and its burden on taxpayers is minor. From this come the following policy ideas:

- **More public borrowing for investment and current expenditure** is technically justified by the size of the debt.
- At the time of the 2010 General Election the share of foreign ownership of the UK debt was 15.6 per cent. Under the coalition and Conservative governments foreign ownership rose in 2018 to 27 per cent of the total. The minor burden represented by foreign interest payments could be reduced by **measures that would limit gilt sales to domestic buyers** (applied in several other countries).
- While interest payments to domestic gilt holders are not a net burden to taxpayers, they may have a negative redistribution effect. This could be eliminated through **progressive income taxation**.
- Should a government face speculative pressure on gilt rates, this could be prevented by **bond sales to the Bank of England or to the proposed public sector investment bank** that some have proposed (creation of such a bank was proposed in the Labour Party's manifesto for the 2017 General Election).

# POLICY IDEA 7

# The macroeconomic role of progressive taxation

*John Weeks*

**What's the issue?**

Capitalist economies tend to instability, 'boom and bust'. An active fiscal policy can moderate that instability with short-term spending and taxation measures (see Policy idea 2, this part). Those measures will be more effective if policies reduce the systemic instability of the private economy.

> **How can tax policy be used to reduce the instability of the private economy?**

**Analysis**

The common perception of taxation is that it serves to fund expenditures. While that is correct to an extent (see Policy idea 2, this part), taxation has at least two other major functions. It can serve as a vehicle of social policy to affect the distribution of income in society. In Britain the distribution of household income after deduction of taxes is considerably more equitable than pre-tax income. Statistics from the Office for National Statistics (ONS) show that for the fiscal year 2016/17 the pre-tax ratio of the richest fifth of the population to the poorest fifth was 12:1. The after-tax ratio fell by almost half, to 6.4:1.

The inequality-reducing effect of the tax system plays an important role in stabilising the economy. If a tax system is progressive, tax revenue increases more than national income increases and vice-versa. Statistics from the ONS monthly report *Public Sector Finances* show that during 2011–17, when the Conservative Chancellor reduced the progressivity of the tax structure, the average rate of change of public revenue remained significantly above the rate of change of GDP. The ratio of the former (rate of revenue change) to the latter (rate of GDP change) is known as the 'income elasticity of revenue'.

That real-world behaviour relationship has a direct impact on the stability of our economy. When a recession hits, business income falls, leading to a fall in business profits, income and private employment. The fall in employment provokes households to reduce their spending as some suffer unemployment and wages tend to fall for those still holding jobs. Household retrenchment of consumption spending adds to, or multiplies, the fall in business investment. If the tax system is progressive, household after-tax income, disposable income, falls less than pre-tax income, leaving more income for consumption expenditures. Pre-tax and after-tax refer to income tax only.

Progressive taxation provides our economy with an 'automatic stabiliser', a built-in cushion that reduces the severity of recession. It also works the other way. When the economy expands, tax rises faster, dampening inflationary pressures that consumption increases might provoke. The more progressive the income tax system, the stronger the automatic stabilising mechanism. Indirect or consumption taxes such as VAT substantially reduce the progressivity of the overall tax system. ONS statistics show that, for all non-retired households, indirect taxes accounted for 20 per cent of their disposable income. For the poorest fifth of the population, the share was 26 per cent and for the richest fifth only 13 per cent.

## What can we do?

In addition to its inequality-reducing effect, a progressive rate structure for income tax provides an important automatic stabiliser for our economy, reducing the severity of recessions and moderating inflationary pressures. A progressive government that seeks to render our economy more stable should apply the following policy ideas:

- Provisions of the tax code permitting **tax avoidance** – provisions available only to the wealthiest fifth of the population – **should be eliminated**, to the extent possible.
- With tax avoidance substantially reduced, **marginal tax rates should be raised, and tax bands or brackets increased in number**. For example, progressively rising rates might apply to incomes at £50,000, £100,000 and £500,000. Each higher rate would apply above the threshold, not below.
- **Revenue from indirect taxes, especially VAT, should be progressively replaced by income tax revenue.** Some indirect taxation would remain in as far as it served a clear social policy purpose.

# POLICY IDEA 8

# How do we build a fairer tax system?

*Richard Murphy*

**What's the issue?**

Tax is an effective tool available to governments to implement their social and economic policies. The current institution for collecting taxes in Britain, Her Majesty's Revenue & Customs (HMRC), does not allow effective use of the tax instrument.

> How should tax administration be administered to ensure accountability, transparency and effectiveness?

**Analysis**

HMRC is not directly accountable to the government. There is no minister with direct responsibility for taxation, nor is there a select committee on taxation in the House of Commons. These missing institutions leave tax administration without sufficient political oversight and with too narrow a mandate, flaws compounded by an invalid presumption that HMRC operates in an apolitical manner.

Under the present system HMRC is apolitical in form but not in practice. The Treasury manages the national budget in ways that, in effect, treat tax functions as a constraint on, rather than a facilitator of, social and economic policy. In addition, the absence of an Office for Tax Responsibility function is a serious shortcoming in Britain – such institutions are common in other developed countries. To make the tax system democratically accountable, Parliament should transform HMRC into a Ministry of Tax, allocating sufficient resources to ensure effective monitoring of tax collection and its social and economic impact.

## What can we do?

- To achieve a tax system that is adequate for implementing progressive policies, the following changes are required. First, **the Cabinet needs a minister responsible for taxation**. This minister's role would be different from that of the Chancellor of the Exchequer, whose principal function is overall economic management.
- Second, because of the importance of taxation, **the Ministry of Tax should operate in cooperation with, but independent of, the Treasury**. The new Ministry would set tax policy to meet the economic objectives set by the Chancellor, who would have overall responsibility for economic policy. The new Ministry would be responsible for facilitating these policies in a transparent manner. The Ministry of Tax would have oversight of revenue collection. A clear division between the Treasury and the Ministry of Tax is essential in order that tax serves its supportive function, assisting the achievement of economic goals rather than functioning as a constraint on them.
- Third, in order **to ensure that the narrow task of tax collection is independent of political influence, the Ministry of Tax would devolve this function to a purely administrative agency**. This is currently the formal task of HMRC, whose name would be altered to emphasise its accountably to Parliament.

- Fourth, **the minister and the Ministry of Tax must be politically accountable**, as are other government ministers. This will require that Parliament has a select committee on tax.
- Fifth, to ensure that the committee has the resources to do its job properly and transparently, **Parliament should create an Office for Tax Responsibility that reports directly to the select committee on taxation**. This Office for Tax Responsibility would have four responsibilities. It would:
  - act as the internal auditor of HMRC;
  - audit the government's tax proposals to verify their credibility;
  - review all allowances and relief in the tax system on a regular basis and recommend changes if any fail to achieve their stated purpose; and
  - audit the 'tax gap', which is the difference between the amount of tax that should be paid each year and the amount actually collected, and report to Parliament on progress in addressing this issue.

As a result of these policies, the UK would, for the first time, have an accountable tax system.

# POLICY IDEA 9

# Should we have fiscal rules?

*Jeremy Smith*

## What's the issue?

Over the last 25 years, governments have become subject to some type of 'fiscal rule' for the management of public finances. Such rules set limits on government debt or budget deficits, or establish targets for reducing public debt and/or deficits.

Are 'fiscal rules' for public debt and budget deficits beneficial tools for controlling or helping elected governments in managing public finances?

## Analysis

Since the early 1990s, a substantial group of economists have argued in favour of a macroeconomic management approach in which public finances should be legally or institutionally constrained, and the role of technocratic input in budget decisions increased.

One favoured principle in this approach is that central banks be independent of government influence or control in relation to monetary policy.

A second holds that governments be constrained by legal or self-imposed 'fiscal rules', which set limits on budget deficits or public debt as a share of GDP, and/or set targets for ongoing reductions. Some countries have also set up technocratic monitoring bodies known as 'fiscal councils'. In the UK, the Office for Budget Responsibility (OBR) plays this role.

This policy of controlling or reducing governmental powers in economic and fiscal management has coincided with the period of financial liberalisation and deregulation. Prior to 1980, budget deficits tended to be low, with borrowing largely for capital investment. During the 1980s and 1990s, however, many economies' deficits grew faster than their GDP, leading to a higher level of debt as a percentage of GDP.

## Deficit bias

The principal purpose of fiscal rules is to combat 'deficit bias' on the part of governments. However, some arguing for hard fiscal rules have an ulterior political motivation – to reduce the size and role of government and public services. For them, the answer is almost always to cut public spending rather than raise taxation.

Many mainstream economists consider deficits the mark of 'bad' governments, acting against their citizens' best interests. Deficit bias arises, they believe, from a willingness to yield to interest groups and push the burden on to future governments and generations.

But there is huge variation across time and between and within countries at different times. In reality, deficits arise from specific political and economic circumstances, not least an economic system prone to financial crises.

The current danger facing many advanced economies arises more from a 'surplus bias', expressed, for example, in the budget 'balanced or in surplus' rule, which Eurozone states signed up to in 2012. Such rules risk deepening recessions, since they require austerity measures to meet their harsh requirements.

## It's the overall economy that matters

A weakness of fiscal rules is the focus on just one aspect of the overall economy. For example, in the lead-up to the financial crisis of 2007–08, public debt-to-GDP ratios were stable or falling. The crisis, caused by private sector excesses and mismanagement, reduced government revenues and saw social expenditure rise (through 'automatic stabilisers'), and many governments took on private finance liabilities (via 'bailouts') to prevent further economic and social collapse.

A narrow focus on reducing deficits or debt can damage the economy – and make the fiscal target harder to reach. If there is slack in the economy, shrinking the public sector will lower economic activity and output. In such cases, deficit reduction targets via public spending cuts may lead to lower GDP – so that the 'cuts' have to be increased further to meet the target. This is what happened in the Eurozone and UK under austerity.

Conversely, maintaining public service expenditure in the aftermath of crisis may speed private economic recovery, so that even if the nominal value of debt increases, as a percentage of GDP it declines.

## Fiscal rules – the UK experience

In 1998, the New Labour government first introduced formalised fiscal rules into the UK, committing itself to the 'golden rule' that current budget spending should be matched by income over the economic cycle, with borrowing permitted for capital spending (investment) only.

Between 1997 and 2007, UK public debt was around 44 per cent of GDP, but as a result of the 2008 crisis, caused by private sector mismanagement, deficits and debt soared. This led, in pre-election political panic, to the UK's most prescriptive fiscal rules, the short-lived Fiscal Responsibility Act 2010.

Since the 2010 coalition government, the UK's 'rules' have been set out in a series of statutory Charters for Budget Responsibility. The 2011 mandate set a target of current budget balance, allowing borrowing for investment.

But in 2015 the Conservative government changed tack, proposing that henceforth all future governments should commit to achieving an *overall* budget surplus, a target that would be suspended if the OBR advised there was 'a significant negative shock'.

Chancellor Hammond's latest version of the Charter drops the aim to run a surplus, and instead aims to reduce the deficit (to below 2 per cent of GDP by 2020–21) and the public debt-to-GDP ratio, with the government aiming 'to return the public finances to balance at the earliest possible date in the next Parliament'.

### The Labour Party 'rule'

Since 2016 the Labour Party has also committed itself to a set of 'rules': (1) targeting 'balance on current spending after a rolling, five-year period'; (2) retaining 'the ability to borrow for investing in capital projects which over time will pay for themselves', seeing this as essential to future prosperity; and (3) reducing government debt as a proportion of 'trend GDP' by the end of each Parliament.

In case of severe economic difficulties, a Labour government would 'reserve the right, for as long as monetary policy is unable to undertake its usual role due to the lower bound, [to] suspend our targets so that monetary and fiscal policy can work together'.

Any suspension of the rule must be authorised by the Bank of England's Monetary Policy Committee.

This formulation is the subject of vigorous debate. Why wait in crisis for the 'lower bound' to be reached? Why should monetary and fiscal measures not be put to work in tandem from the outset?

Both monetary and fiscal policies, depending on circumstances, have their specific roles and limitations; the art is to combine them effectively. In the US, the Economic Stimulus Act was passed in February 2008 – at peak crisis – when the Fed's federal funds rate was still at 3 per cent. In the severe early 1990s recession, interest rates never got close to the 'lower bound'.

## What can we do?

- Fiscal rules vary from those that are legally enforceable to those that are, in essence, political commitments.
- A monetary union (a special case) may indeed need some 'backstop' enforceable rules, but these should not be as constrictive as the present ones, which require budgets to always be in balance or surplus.
- Rules also face the weakness that governments that share their policy goal do not need them, while governments that do not agree with the goal will either change the rule, find ways of avoiding it in practice – or, worse, bring in harmful policies just to stick to the letter of the rule.
- The case for fiscal rules has weakened since 2008. For most advanced economies, interest rates have stayed low, and debt interest payments as a share of GDP are at historic lows, despite nominal debt rising.
- Where arguably inappropriate deficits exist, enforcement of a strict rule would almost certainly be regressive – targeting social spending for the poor, rather than higher taxes for the rich. Fears that 'excessive' fiscal deficits will lead to inflation, or 'crowding out' of private sector investment, have proven far wide of the mark.
- Even the 'golden rule' (borrow for investment only) suffers from the problem that the capital/current borderline (set out in accounting rules) does not help in deciding what spending is, in fact, for long-term benefit. For example, much education and health 'current' spending will benefit future generations, though it is as much on staff (teachers, nurses) as on buildings and equipment (see Part Two, Policy idea 6).

**Fiscal rules are dysfunctional instruments for successful economic management, and should be avoided.**

**In place of such 'rules', there should be full transparency of the government's main economic objectives and assumptions.** At the outset of their term and annually, governments should provide a public, unified statement of key macroeconomic and public finance objectives, with changes being explained in annual updates. The statement would set out (1) the government's economic objectives/targets, and (2) the main assumptions that underpin its policy. These may vary; one government may have a primary policy objective for unemployment, while another may prioritise inflation, GDP per capita, etc.

This statement thus forms the basis for a *democratic* accountability for economic management in the round.

**When events cause a government to change (or miss) its key objectives or targets, this is a matter for political explanation and debate**, not legal sanction, and its assumptions or targets for the public finances will be placed in their broader economic context, not simply as narrow 'fiscal rules'.

**A role remains for bodies such as the OBR in offering an external interpretation of government finances and assumptions**, provided it does not take the form of policy *control*. But a proposal to give another body power to decide whether government may use fiscal policy in a crisis should be rejected outright on grounds of democratic principle.

# Interlude: Has privatisation come off the rails?

Sue Konzelmann and Marc Fovargue-Davies

The idea of privatisation of state-owned assets – such as energy, water and rail services – was originally 'sold' to us on the basis of more choice, better services and lower costs. A few decades on, it looks like these have entirely failed to materialise. Is that because privatisation is always a bad idea? Or is it because there were very good reasons why many services were state-run monopolies in the first place?

Choice is hardly a factor in rail travel, for example. Whether we're racing for the evening commute or going to visit friends and family, we just get on the train that's going the right direction at the right time – just like we always did. We do get a change of operator when moving between franchise areas, but that's hardly a cause for joy. Then, of course, there are the regular rows over fare increases well beyond inflation, slow and inconsistent upgrades – and, of course, operating companies' profits – to consider. As things stand, operating companies have to guess how much profit they'll make. If they make less, the government tops it up, and if they make more, they pay the government back. This creates an obvious temptation to exaggerate profit forecasts, and profit is not all reinvested.

These problems aren't unique to rail. While not all of us use the network, very few can avoid dealing with the energy sector. Along with housing, both main political parties have routinely described the energy market as 'broken' – so what's wrong with it?

The bulk of the electricity and gas market in the UK is supplied by the 'Big Six' energy companies, whose job it is – in theory, at least – to deliver the choice, keen pricing and better service that we were promised. But, once again, the reality is that, in spite of regular encouragement by services like uSwitch, two-thirds of energy users have never switched supplier. Not only does this mean that 'more choice' has again eluded the majority of us; it turns out that these loyal customers are also paying more than they should, helping to maintain suppliers' profits. An obvious conclusion from this might be that those who are not switching are simply enjoying the improved service that they were promised.

Predictably, however, this doesn't stand up either: in terms of customer satisfaction, the 'Big Six' make a fairly dismal showing in the uSwitch customer ratings, with small, specialist companies consistently monopolising the top spots.

The reality is that most of us have little choice but to use essential nationwide services such as rail, public utilities and services like the NHS. If these are privatised, the focus will inevitably be on profit rather than service level – and that really isn't a good idea when these services are at the heart of our wellbeing – not to mention that of the economy.

Some things are natural state monopolies. Big services need an equally big vision, and, yes, big money. However, as a certain TV ad succinctly puts it, 'We're worth it…'.

# Part Two: Public investment – Prioritising society rather than profit

## Introduction

*Sue Konzelmann and Marc Fovargue-Davies*

Following the financial crisis in 2008, and fearing that their financial systems would collapse if they didn't, many governments invested huge amounts of public money to resurrect banks deemed 'too big to fail'. But not all. Iceland's banks had grown too big to rescue, with loans amounting to ten times the size of the entire national economy. So, unlike in the UK, the Icelandic banks were allowed to fail, while Iceland prioritised its people over finance. As a result, Iceland today is in far better economic shape than most of the rest of Europe. The message is therefore clear: the state can *choose* what to invest in, what its objectives should be and what form the returns from that investment should take.

Listening to many in the media, as well as free market economists, it is easy to get the impression that the only choice on offer is between the 'free market' policies that produced the present situation and those described as 'hard left', 'Trotskyite' or even 'totalitarian', which apparently failed during the 1970s. But this is a smokescreen that obscures the *real* question: what policies do we need *now*, to address the problems we currently face? Turning the clock back to the 1940s, the 1970s – or, indeed, the 1980s – won't answer that question. A better bet is to look at *new* ideas and *not* to rely on dogma.

New ideas in themselves, however, may not always be enough. They will not have been tried before, so implementing them would, to some degree, be an experiment. For others, there may be something to be learned from economic history. In other words, what happened when similar ideas were tried in the past? What can we learn from this – and what might we do differently this time? Economic history reveals, for example, that much of the programme of nationalisation in Britain, following the Second World War was undermined by failing to look forward and invest in the future. Economic history should also have told former Chancellor George Osborne that austerity during a recession not only makes things worse, economically; it also makes people wonder how things could be done differently.

Looking back, some would argue that, with the changes following the Second World War, there was *too much* state involvement in some parts of the economy – if not society. Equally, it is not difficult to conclude that after 1980, in both the economy and society, there hasn't been anything like enough. However, rather than worrying about the *extent* of state involvement, it makes far more sense to consider its role – after all, there are things that *only* government can do – and what might be the best ways of managing the state's relationship with the public, private and third sectors. In other words, *how* should the state be involved – both now and in the future?

The key to successful socioeconomic progress – and the development of policies for guiding it – is a clear and ambitious vision of the outcomes we want. It has been many years since politicians in the UK spent much time talking about the kind of country and society they want to live in, but without this kind of vision, it's impossible either to make effective plans for change or to resource them realistically. Whatever this vision eventually turns out to be, it's high time to put society back at the top of the agenda – and to start asking the really big question: what kind of place do we want Britain to be – and how do we make it happen?

The 'policy ideas' in this part of the book consider how industrial strategy and policy – together with industrial relations, labour regulation and wage policy – might be redirected to create the conditions supporting not only economic prosperity and sustainable development, but also income and employment security for the many.

The first two policy ideas focus on industrial strategy: Sue Konzelmann and Marc Fovargue-Davies take inspiration from the strategy that not only successfully transformed the international competitiveness of Team GB, following its devastating performance in the 1996 Atlanta Summer Games, but has also delivered continuous improvement ever since. Antonio Andreoni and Ha-Joon Chang consider the UK's latest industrial strategy and what the key elements of a more convincing approach might be. Keith D. Ewing and John Hendy QC propose ways of using labour law to promote a more equal and democratic society. Ideas about how to build a sustainable economy are presented by Özlem Onaran and Dan O'Neill, before we turn to the question of the benefits of investment in social infrastructure – and how it might be used to reduce gender inequalities. Susan Himmelweit considers how the government should invest in R&D (research and development), while Jeff Tan and Hulya Dagdeviren explore ideas about nationalising critical public services, including railways and energy.

## Policy ideas

1. How could we build competitive new UK industries? *Sue Konzelmann and Marc Fovargue-Davies*
2. Reindustrialising the UK *Antonio Andreoni and Ha-Joon Chang*
3. How can labour law be the instrument of progressive economic policy? *Keith D. Ewing and John Hendy QC*
4. Wage policy and public investment for sustainable development *Özlem Onaran*
5. How do we build a sustainable economy? *Dan O'Neill*
6. Investing in social infrastructure *Susan Himmelweit*
7. Why should the railway be renationalised? *Jeff Tan*
8. How can we fix the broken energy sector? *Hulya Dagdeviren*

# How could we build competitive new UK industries?

*Sue Konzelmann and Marc Fovargue-Davies*

## What's the issue?

Much has been made of the UK 'jobs miracle' since 2010, but many are low-paid, insecure jobs that not only need supplementary benefits to become a living wage, but also contribute to low productivity.

> Building competitive new industries would create more, more secure – and better-paid – jobs, improving both society and productivity, but how do we do it?

## Analysis

*A new partnership between government and industry*

Neither the UK's previous approach to nationalised industry nor the complete lack of interest by governments since 1980 helped industry thrive. Fortunately, these two extremes aren't the only choices available. Instead, the state and industrial organisations could work together, each contributing its own special skills – resulting in a much 'smarter' policy.

This might sound optimistic, but such cooperation already happens – and the UK can be incredibly good at it. The best example, so far at least, was initiated by a Conservative Prime Minister – and improved by the following Labour one – showing that politicians can indeed work successfully with organisations outside government. The transformation of the international competitiveness of Team GB – from zeroes in 1996 to the heroes they are today – offers clear insight into more effective industrial policy design.

If you look at the system that has been developed around the Department for Digital, Culture, Media & Sport's (DCMS) 'arm's-length' operation, UK Sport, as an industrial sector that produces successful world-class athletes, its relevance to UK industry is hard to ignore.

Not only is this elite sport system highly successful, it was also born during a recession and following the British Olympic team's worst-ever performance in 1996. That leaves little excuse for not designing and implementing a proper industrial strategy now.

Nothing would have changed for Team GB, however, without government backing. This came in the form of the then Prime Minister John Major, who recognised sport's political value. In 1996, neither UK elite sport nor industry was getting much state support – to the point where Team GB cyclists, who now dominate the sport, even had to hand back their singlets so that others could use them in future events. Team GB was chronically underfunded, not just looking for Mr Hammond's now notorious 'little extras'. It took a bespoke solution – the National Lottery – also backed by John Major, to begin the change, with elite sport being one of the 'good causes' eligible for funding.

Likewise, a specialist solution will be necessary to supply adequate, stable and competitive funding to industry rather than leaving things to the whims of a capricious market. It's significant that almost every other developed nation – except the UK – has a business investment bank.

Public funding must also be properly accounted for; corporate governance at sport governing bodies was therefore vastly improved, making them far more efficient in the use of those extra funds, which were invested in a constantly developing system to produce and maintain competitiveness. But on its own, money is not enough to drive change.

## It's not just about the money

Both politicians and the media routinely put Team GB's success down purely to the increased funding. But, while the transformation would not have been possible without it, as many Premier League football managers have discovered, money – even in far larger quantities than the funds distributed by UK Sport – is no guarantee of success. UK Sport's cost per medal is actually lower than some of its less successful competitors.

The creation of UK Sport as the strategic lead body was crucial for the effective investment of the extra funds. As an 'arm's-length' public body, it is accountable to both government and the rest of the elite sport network. It is run by ex-athletes, who know rather more about winning medals at the highest level, rather than by civil servants. Along with a more connected network of relationships, UK Sport brought a vision. It was ambitious, but the leadership was also there to help make it a reality, moving Team GB from 15 medals and 36th place in 1996 to 67 medals and 2nd in 2016. British industry, too, will need a step-change in vision and leadership to drive a significant transformation – as well as the appropriate resources.

## Government must be actively involved – but quality relationships are crucial

The initial lack of funding wasn't the only problem elite sport had – the rules on what it could be spent on were also undermining success. It could only buy facilities – so Team GB athletes would be underprepared – albeit in a great stadium.

While government leaves the technical side of delivering Olympic medals to those parts of the network best able to do that, sporting organisations can't change the legal framework, although they can talk to government about it – who can make changes. As a result, New Labour made an informed change, allowing money to be spent on anything necessary for success. Equally, effective relationships throughout the network to identify talent, develop it through world-class training and deal with any problems quickly help to make that happen. The quality of the relationship between government and non-governmental organisations (NGOs) is therefore a critical success factor. DCMS, UK Sport and the various sport governing bodies work together, rather than independently, with a forward-looking strategic view – something that nationalised British industries typically lacked – minimising unexpected difficulties.

For UK industry, this kind of alliance with government will be at least as important as adequate funding and training. Again, only government can make legal changes to the business environment, making a 'hands-off' approach by government irrational at best. The current legal framework makes it very difficult for small independent businesses to cooperate. This limits productive relationships and the rebuilding of the UK's business 'ecosystem', and has clear implications for industrial strategy.

## Picking winners? Not really

While post-war nationalisation often propped up ailing industries, UK Sport initially focused on those sports with a reasonable chance of success – effectively, the winners chose themselves. But, as systems for identifying and developing talent have improved, Team GB can now win medals in sports where the UK has no previous record of success, such as gymnastics and diving. It is again reasonable to argue that both of these things would probably also be true in industry – especially as new technologies offering new opportunities seem to be a regular fact of life.

## The crucial role of cultural context

The UK, however, didn't invent elite sport strategy. Instead – and as we still do in industry – Britain had to compete against those who did, but without any strategy at all. It's therefore hardly surprising that we were going backwards. Even so, the UK didn't simply copy the Australian or former Soviet systems. Instead, we took inspiration from those systems, but developed a peculiarly British version, based mostly on existing organisations, and focused on UK requirements, in a UK cultural context. Which is partly why it works so well.

So, while inspiration for an industrial development model might well come from obvious industrial leaders like Germany or South East Asia, any attempt to simply transplant a system would probably result in failure – such as the attempt to import US methods during the 1960s and 1970s. A successful UK industrial strategy should be founded mostly on existing industry bodies, businesses, colleges and universities, in a UK cultural context – but with a strategic lead body performing a comparable function to UK Sport.

## What can we do?

Key components of a system for developing international industrial competitiveness should include:

- **A compelling vision for the future of UK industry.**
- **Resources** (money, business services, training and support) to implement it.
- **A new strategic lead body** for industry – run by business people – to provide leadership, help set goals, allocate resources and manage the relationship with government.
- **Improve the relationships** between industry bodies, businesses, universities and colleges. Where **essential training** is not available, it should be provided.
- Change the league table criteria in schools to put **more emphasis on technical training**.
- **Improve the image of industry.** It can be a very exciting environment, often with spectacular results. We should celebrate that – and inspire more young people.

# POLICY IDEA 2

# Reindustrialising the UK

*Antonio Andreoni and Ha-Joon Chang*

**What's the issue?**

The UK economy is at a crossroads. Following on from the dramatic deindustrialisation that began in the 1970s, and the increasing loss of global industrial competitiveness from the late 1990s, today's UK industrial sector is a pale shadow of its former self. Since the global financial crisis, all governments have recognised the need for an industrial strategy to rebalance the UK economy (both sectorally and regionally), improve its productivity, and enable it to reap the benefits of the green technology transition and the digital industrial revolution.

In 2017, the Conservative government launched a new industrial strategy and, after several months, an Industrial Strategy Council was set up, chaired by Andy Haldane, chief economist of the Bank of England.

Given the UK's modest track record in industrial strategy, and the mounting challenge of reindustrialising the economy in the face of intense international competition, the extent to which the latest strategy is up to the challenge has been widely questioned.

**What then, should the key elements of a more convincing approach actually be?**

## Analysis

Since 1998, the UK has experienced a fall in its global share of all major manufacturing industries. This loss has been only partially compensated by growth in the business services sectors. These, of course, were also badly hit by the financial crisis (see Figures 4 and 5 below) and the impact of Brexit remains unclear. Deindustrialisation has also brought a drop in productivity – especially among small and medium-sized enterprises (SMEs) and service companies. Meanwhile, 'financialisation' – the increasing pressure on manufacturing companies to deliver higher short-term profits for shareholders – has also meant that R&D (research and development) and fixed capital investments have been slashed. All this has resulted in the polarisation and disarticulation of the UK's industrial ecosystem; combined with a decade of austerity, this has also had a dramatic – and negative – impact on the fortunes of communities and regions that rely on manufacturing.

In response to this, as well as mounting competition from both low-cost economies at one end of the market (such as China) and high-tech economies at the other (like the US, Germany, Japan and Korea), the UK government has at last rediscovered the need for an industrial strategy. This, however, has also revealed the UK's lack of institutions needed for industrial development, for policy coordination across government departments, and for the alignment of interests across sectors. Without addressing this, it is very doubtful whether an industrial policy can be properly implemented.

**Figure 4:** Global value-added by UK manufacturers

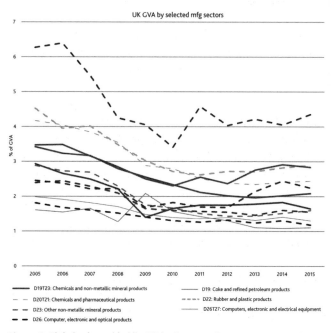

**Figure 5:** Global value-added by UK business services

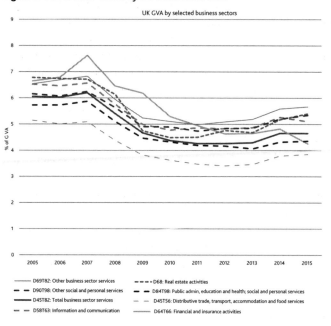

## What can we do?

From this brief analysis, the basic areas that will need to be dramatically improved – and which will then form the key elements of an effective industrial strategy – are not hard to identify:

- **Rebuild the UK's industrial ecosystems.** After decades of promoting innovation without production, it is time to rebuild industrial ecosystems around university knowledge hubs and promote the renewal of regions across the country. The current local economic partnerships (LEPs) do not effectively map out location-specific opportunities or address the growing polarisation of SMEs and large firms. To rebuild industrial ecosystems, sectoral relationships and supply chains must be nurtured.
- **Reimagine industrial policy instruments.** After decades without an industrial policy at all, the debate in the UK is still being framed by policy ideas that are at least four decades out of date. On the one hand, there are the supporters of the free market who remain opposed to the active involvement of an 'entrepreneurial' state (a view that has brought us to the present position), and on the other, are the 'old-style interventionists' whose idea of industrial policy instruments is largely limited to subsidies. The latter have claimed that European Union (EU) law has limited industrial policy space, but this completely ignores the range of policies that other EU member states such as Germany and France are already using to good effect. These range from basic instruments, such as skills development policy, to the rather sexier – but equally obvious – promotion of emerging technology sectors.
- **Restructure industrial policy and governance.** The increasingly systemic nature of manufacturing industries calls for efficient coordination across government departments and agencies, to deliver an industrial policy. The recent establishment of a dedicated committee is not enough, as the UK industrial policy governance structure is still not up to the job of handling the complex tasks ahead. With this lack of industrial policy infrastructure, reindustrialisation will

require government branches – insatiably at least – to focus on a limited number of sectors for intervention.

- **Rewrite the rules of creation, capture and retention of economic value.** Corporate governance reforms to address the increasing financialisation of the manufacturing sector are critical to success. These reforms need to support value creation, capture and retention, rather than short-term shareholder value. The UK has a poor record in this, especially in its attitude to new models involving workers in business enterprise governance; this is increasingly important, with the ever-growing complexity of manufacturing. Meeting this challenge – as well as others posed by transnational corporations (such as the so-called 'GAFA' – Google, Apple, Facebook and Amazon) – should be a key goal of industrial strategy, as success (or otherwise) will determine investment dynamics, innovation and the creation of good employment opportunities.

- **Forge an alliance between manufacturers against 'rentier' interests.** An industrial strategy is neither just a collection of policies nor simply a solution to a technical problem. It must provide a clearly articulated vision to align the productive forces of the economy, across both the public and private sectors. Not only does this help rebuild the economic ecosystem, it is also an unmistakable statement as to how the roles of the 'real' and financial sectors of the economy are intended to function. At the moment, the 'rentier' sector – effectively, finance – has excessive power, which, if not addressed, would soon undermine both the competitiveness and social sustainability of an effective industrial strategy. Business organisations are part of the solution to rebuilding the UK's industrial base and rebalancing the economy – and tackling the high and growing inequality in British society requires the creation of much improved employment opportunities, and innovative and productive organisations.

# POLICY IDEA 3

# How can labour law be the instrument of progressive economic policy?

*Keith D. Ewing and John Hendy QC*

**What's the issue?**

What is the role of labour law in promoting a more equal and democratic society? By a more equal society we mean one in which the current inequalities of income and power are greatly diminished. By a more democratic society, we mean one in which citizens as workers are integrated through their trade unions in the decisions that affect their working lives.

It is a well-worn aphorism that democracy does not begin and end at the ballot box every five years or at the whim of an incumbent Prime Minister. It is a principle that applies to all aspects of life, but most especially to working life, where we are subject to the governance and rules of others. Where there is disparity of power it needs to be confronted and redressed.

For most people it is the employer who has the greatest power over their lives, although we do not discount the power of the state or the landlord. But it is employer power that determines not only the rules of the workplace, but also the quality of life for workers and their families outside work. The employers' power to determine pay determines where we live, what we can spend our free time on, and whether, where and how often we go on holiday.

The challenge for labour law is how to give workers voice – in government, in industry and in the corporation – in a way that socialises power through participation in decision-making. This political dimension – empowerment and equal participation – of the case for labour reinforces what we readily acknowledge to be the social and economic case that has already been made effectively by scholars in other disciplines.

**What is the role of labour law in promoting a more equal and democratic society?**

## Analysis

*Socialising industry*

The starting point is a new social agenda for industry, by the reordering of collective bargaining on a sectoral basis. Sectoral collective bargaining is a practice that we are very familiar with in the UK, having been actively promoted by governments from the 1930s until the 1970s. Its main effect is to raise the levels of collective bargaining coverage – more workers are covered by a collective agreement as a result, with workers' terms and conditions improved accordingly.

Extensive collective bargaining coverage requires the active intervention of the state, which, in the 20th century, was undertaken by the Ministry of Labour and its successors. In those days it was possible for the government to rely on crude administrative power to persuade or coerce employers to participate in such arrangements, only occasionally having to fall back on legislative mechanisms such as the Wages Councils Acts to establish wage-setting structures.

That approach would not be possible today, and as the Institute of Employment Rights has proposed, we now need a Collective Bargaining Act that would require the creation of National Joint Councils (NJCs) on an industry by industry basis to establish minimum terms and conditions of employment for all workers in the industry concerned. As the Institute points out, such legislation will have to address a range of difficult questions, such as identifying the scope of each sector, and dealing with the problem of employer non-cooperation in the sense of refusal to participate.

Other questions that would have to be addressed are the questions of trade union competition (where there is more than one union in any sector); the scope of the bargaining agenda (the Institute has a comprehensive list of 41 items); and the question of enforcement of NJC agreements. Also important would be the need to respect existing sectoral structures where they exist, as well as enterprise bargaining arrangements currently in force. But it is important to emphasise that sectoral and enterprise bargaining are complementary.

But in governance terms, one of the main aims and consequences of sectoral collective bargaining (SCB) is to restore the legitimacy of trade unions as regulatory bodies – democratically based organisations that make the rules or participate in making the rules on behalf of workers collectively. With the attack on SCB since the early 1980s, that role has gone, with trade unions assigned a role by neoliberalism that is at best a representative one. Representing members' interests is clearly an important function of trade unions. But the ambition needs to be greater.

## Socialising the corporation

The socialisation of the economy does not end with industry. It must also include the corporation. That need will be met to some extent by enterprise collective bargaining, which we see as continuing in the shadow of SCB, to supplement the terms of NJC agreements and to render the latter more relevant in their application in particular enterprises. To this end, it would be necessary to heavily amend the existing trade union recognition legislation to make it easier for trade unions to deal with hostile employers.

But that is not enough. The Institute's *Manifesto for Labour Law* (see www.ier/org.uk/manifesto) made three main proposals for worker participation in companies. These were:

- to require that directors owe duties to 'enhance and protect the interests of workers [as they do towards] shareholders';
- 'Every board must have worker directors [who] should be appointed by recognised trade unions (or, in the absence of representative unions, elected worker representatives)'; and
- 'Workers through their trade union should have a minimum percentage of the vote in general meetings of the company'.

The *Manifesto* left for later consideration the 'detail of the proportions, exemptions and application to related entities'. That said, it proposed that worker directors and votes in the general meeting should be channelled principally through trade unions. It is essential that it is union candidates who represent workers on boards, and that union delegates are able to organise collectively workers' votes in general meetings. This would achieve consistency with union policy in future sectoral collective agreements.

Socialisation of the corporation has another consequence beyond votes and participation in decision-making. There is also the question of worker capital in the form of pension funds, on the vulnerability of which to corporate abuse we are regularly reminded by recurring scandals. This is workers' money and should be controlled by workers themselves through their trade unions. With workers having a democratic voice in their pensions, we will move towards a truly democratic economy in which trade unions have real power.

Finally, we consider that attention should be given to the greatest exemption from the rule of law yet achieved by capitalism, that of limited liability. This is the legal device by which directors and shareholders evade all personal liability for the wrongdoing of the entity they control and fund, and from which they often extract great wealth. Too often this has been used to defeat the interests of workers and others, and its limits merit full consideration at a later date.

## What can we do?

- A new settlement requires **a new department to represent the voice of labour in government**. Workers' interests are currently represented by the Department for Business, Energy and Industrial Strategy (BEIS), workers' interests always subordinate to those of business. The current departmental structure in Whitehall reflects the idea of a community of interest between business and labour: what is good for business is good for labour.

- Proponents of a restored **Ministry for Labour** are usually confronted with the claim that it would take too long to create, and that we should work with existing structures. To which the reply is that new departments can be created overnight by delegated legislation. And, as for working with existing structures, we need a root-and-branch culture change so that labour interests do not continue to be infected by the neoliberal virus prevalent for so long.

- Here we would be retracing big steps taken in the past, a Ministry of Labour having once been a feature of British government. First created by Lloyd George in 1916 in response to trade union demands, the functions of the Ministry under Labour and coalition governments were made clear by the appointment as leading trade unionists Secretaries of State to provide political leadership, including Ernest Bevin, Transport and General Workers Union (TGWU) General Secretary.

- If labour law is to become the instrument of radical change, it will thus need a new Ministry of Labour at the heart of government with a **Secretary of State equal in rank at least to their Business counterpart**. That department will sit at the heart of a complex structure, coordinating workers' interests with HM Treasury, BEIS (if it is retained in its present form), the Department for Education, the Department for Work and Pensions (if it survives) and the Ministry of Justice.

- **To that department should be transferred a wide range of responsibilities**, including wages, working conditions, skills and training, health and safety, pensions and international labour standards, as well as oversight of a properly resourced Labour Inspectorate. But without the proper structures in place and an active minister to push for change, the delivery of progressive economics will always lag behind the ambition of its authors. This is essential.

## POLICY IDEA 4

# Wage policy and public investment for sustainable development

*Özlem Onaran*

**What's the issue?**

Since 1980, obsessively market-based policies have given Britain very high levels of inequality, as well as the worst investment and productivity record in the developed world. Reconstructing this broken system will require a set of policies based on public investment, plus labour market policies for equality-led growth – and a more bounded role for markets.

> How can we effectively address high inequality, low investment and poor productivity?

**Analysis**

Stagnant wages, caused by decades of attacks on trade unions, zero-hours contracts, self-employment practices and public sector cuts and pay freezes, have led to high household debt – and the unsustainable British debt-led consumption-driven growth model. Higher – and smarter – public investment is the key to producing better jobs, reducing inequality and supporting ecological and social sustainability. This will require well-planned, green physical infrastructure, as well as systems supporting social care, health, education and childcare.

Green physical infrastructure priorities should include renewable energy, public transport, social housing and the improvement of the existing housing stock. Investment in health and social care, education and childcare will have long-term benefits for society – improving productivity by supporting a higher-skilled and healthier labour force.

Improving gender equality would also increase productivity, as a result of more women joining the paid labour force. Spending on universal health and social care, education and childcare could be financed by both borrowing and tax revenues, since it adds to valuable – and productive – social infrastructure. Both the Organisation for Economic Co-operation and Development (OECD) and the International Monetary Fund (IMF) support borrowing for public infrastructure investment, particularly as interest rates are currently low.

The public spending and investment priorities in the 2017 Labour Party manifesto were criticised on the assumption that progressive taxation of income, wealth and corporate profits to provide finance for public spending would reduce private investment and productivity. But this view totally ignores the positive impact these policies would have on demand, productivity and, thus, private investment, and it is one of the ideas that produced the problems we now have. But it is not the only one. Current policy is based on two further ideas, both of which are also highly suspect. The first is the notion that a further decrease in the corporate tax rate will somehow be the magic bullet to solve our productivity puzzle. The second is the equally unfounded idea that low wages and labour market deregulation are somehow key to stimulating private investment.

The evidence debunks both of these ideas. Despite – or, more likely, because of – decreasing corporate tax rates and rising profits since the 1980s, Britain has one of the lowest levels of productivity and private investment within the developed world. Increased profits have failed to produce matching private investment, which itself responds to both demand and public infrastructure, not just to profitability. Reliance on low public spending and low wages has produced a fragile, unstable growth model, based on high household debt, which has also discouraged investment. Rather than investing, companies have exploited low labour costs.

Firms have also increasingly directed profits to financial speculation. The proportion of non-financial corporations' profits going to real investment have declined from about 80 per cent during the 1980s to less than 50 per cent in 2019, while their financial assets have substantially increased. Financial speculation, along with larger dividend payments, has slashed private investment in machinery and equipment. Clearly, instead of lower corporate taxation, we need corporate governance policies that incentivise long-term investment and discourage short-term speculation (for example, higher taxation on non-reinvested profits).

## What can we do?

- Wage growth can both reverse economic fragility and improve domestic demand, stimulating business investment. This requires **labour market policies aimed at: reducing inequalities, targeting all wage levels; improving trade union legislation and collective bargaining coverage; and banning zero-hours contracts and dubious self-employment practices**. It also requires **enforcement of gender equality; a living wage to tackle low pay; an enforced pay ratio between the highest and lowest paid employee in the public sector and in the companies bidding for government contracts; and a high top marginal income tax rate**.
- Such a policy package would have a strong positive impact on growth and private investment as well as government's budget. Higher economic growth produces increases in tax revenues, more than offsetting the higher public spending. The dynamic multiplier effects of public spending, combined with higher wages and more equal income distribution are, of course, ignored by those supporting the policies that have gotten us

into our present position. This is more than a little surprising, given their obsession with markets and GDP growth. Our research puts the multiplier in Britain at about 2.2, so a £1 increase in demand due to public spending or higher wages would produce £2.20 increase in GDP.

## POLICY IDEA 5

# How do we build a sustainable economy?

*Dan O'Neill*

**What's the issue?**

Economic growth is the UK's overall policy goal; Section 108 of the Deregulation Act 2015 requires anyone in a regulatory function to have 'regard to the desirability of promoting economic growth'. However, this is at odds with environmental sustainability, and it isn't necessary for achieving things like full employment or a better quality of life. Even Simon Kuznets, who first developed the indicators of economic growth, warned that an economy should not be managed on this basis. A different philosophy, which prioritises people and the environment rather than an often misleading number, is clearly needed.

**What policies would support a sustainable economy?**

## Analysis

Figure 6 below shows the UK's *material footprint* compared with GDP. This is one of the best environmental pressure indicators available, measuring all the materials required to support consumption, regardless of where they originate. Although it has been suggested that economic activity can be separated from environmental impact ('green growth'), there is little evidence to support the idea. The UK's material footprint has actually increased *faster* than GDP, while globally (especially since 2000), it parallels GDP.

**Figure 6:** Material footprint in comparison to GDP (indexed to 1990)

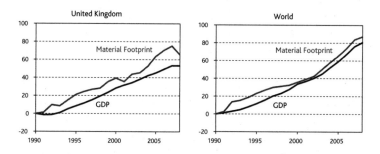

The relationship between GDP and environmental pressure matters, because resource use is already unsustainable. A major 2015 study in the journal *Science* identified nine boundaries essential to the planet's continued equilibrium, four of which – climate change, biodiversity loss, land use change and biogeochemical flows (phosphorus and nitrogen) – had already been crossed. The study concluded that transgressing even one of these boundaries could lead to catastrophic changes.

Even if we found an economic growth strategy that didn't use resources or negatively impact the environment, there is evidence that more growth in wealthy countries might not be worthwhile anyway. Although UK per capita GDP has more than tripled since 1950, its citizens are no more content; surveys of happiness and life satisfaction suggest that – beyond the level required to meet relatively basic needs – additional money does not buy additional happiness. Once those basic needs are met, things like relationships, health, living in a safe community and working in a secure job become more important to wellbeing than more income from extra GDP.

## What can we do?

We should abandon GDP growth as an overarching goal, instead aiming to directly improve quality of life and environmental sustainability. Ecological *macroeconomic models* already exist that explore the changes needed for a sustainable economy. These include:

- **Better measures of progress.** New indicators should replace GDP. Instead of a single indicator, five headline indicators include: (1) the *genuine progress indicator*, an 'adjusted GDP', currently used in the US states of Vermont and Maryland, that adds the value of non-market activity such as household and volunteer work, and deducts the cost of undesirable activity such as crime, pollution and depletion of natural capital; (2) *inequality*, the after-tax income of the top 10 per cent of households in relation to the bottom 10 per cent; (3) *sustainable employment*, the percentage of the labour force with a secure job that pays at least the living wage; (4) *material footprint*, the total quantity of biomass, minerals and fossil fuels required to produce the goods and services consumed in the UK; and (5) *wellbeing*, that is, self-reported life satisfaction.
- **Greater income and wealth equality.** Economic growth is often used as an excuse to avoid addressing poverty and inequality, on the basis that 'a rising tide lifts all boats'. But this has clearly not happened in Britain, with inequality rising markedly since the 1990s. Interventions, such as a universal basic income or universal maximum income, is needed to address this. As a first step, a basic income pilot project could be introduced and maximum pay differentials within government could be set (see Part Three, Policy idea 4; Part Four, Policy ideas 5, 6 and 7). Efforts should also be made to democratise workplaces and encourage cooperatives.

- **Limits on resource use and waste production.** Under a previous Labour government, the UK committed to reduce greenhouse gas emissions by 80 per cent by 2050, addressing one of the nine planetary boundaries – with the other eight remaining outstanding. Resource use and the creation of pollutants should be capped; renewable resources, such as fisheries and forests, should be harvested no faster than they can regenerate; while non-renewables, such as phosphorus, should be used no faster than their waste products can be absorbed.

- **A shorter working week.** Over time, productivity has increased, so the same goods and services can be produced with less labour now than a generation ago. Instead of using this to reduce working hours, we have mostly used it to produce more. However, continually ramping up production while already transgressing four planetary boundaries is clearly unsustainable. We could instead reduce working hours, moving towards a four-day working week. Initially, this might be offered as an option to employees. Aside from more leisure time and better wellbeing, it could help reduce unemployment by sharing available work more equally.

# POLICY IDEA 6

# Investing in social infrastructure

*Susan Himmelweit*

**What's the issue?**

Spending on high-quality public services is one of the best investments that a society can make. With access to such services, children grow up to be better educated, more productive and more contented citizens. Effective public services also boost wellbeing and reduce suffering among adults, preventing a greater need for spending on services in the future. All these are reasons for seeing judicious spending on public services as a worthwhile investment.

Public services, such as education, childcare, health and social care, are also the core of a country's social infrastructure, benefiting the whole society, not only those who are currently using those services. The care system, for example, should be seen as part of our social infrastructure because we all benefit from knowing that proper care will be there for us when we need it. We can also contribute better to society when we are less concerned as to whether those for whom we feel responsible are receiving good quality care.

However, when the government talks of investing in infrastructure, it means spending to build physical infrastructure, power stations, roads or railways, for example. When the aim is to stimulate the economy, investing in social infrastructure is rarely considered, even though it is particularly good at generating new employment opportunities. This bias is not only short-sighted, denying us investment in vital public services; it also increases gender inequalities. The extra jobs generated by constructing physical infrastructure are largely filled by men, whereas the jobs created by investment in social infrastructure are more likely to be filled by women.

> **How can investment in social infrastructure benefit us all and reduce gender inequalities?**

## Analysis

'Investment' means spending money now on producing benefits for the future. Any government spending can stimulate the economy, but it is usually investment spending that is proposed when a stimulus is wanted. In that way the economy gains in two ways: from the longer-term benefits that the investment was designed to provide *and* from higher levels of employment and better use of resources now.

Investment in infrastructure provides even greater benefits, because what's meant by 'infrastructure' is something that provides public good benefits to society as a whole, not just to its immediate users. We are used to thinking of roads, railways and even high-speed internet as infrastructure, but that is also how the health, education and care systems should be seen. These qualify as infrastructure, because it's not just their direct users, such as patients, pupils, pre-school children, people with disabilities and the frail elderly, who benefit from them, but all of us, through having such systems in place. One important feature of infrastructure is that it is always underprovided if its funding is left just to its direct users, because no one then pays for its public good benefits. So adequate provision of infrastructure always requires some state funding.

The case for there being long-term and public good benefits varies between different types of public services. The investment case may appear stronger for education and the care of younger people but, insofar as the care of people of any age brings improvements that are cumulative, and thus improves their longer-term health and wellbeing, at least some portion of expenditure on it should be regarded as an investment. There is also a strong case for seeing reliable systems of care as a public good – allowing everyone to be confident that not only their children and parents, but they themselves, will be looked after well, should the need arise.

The benefits of spending on public services, however, are often underestimated, because it is seen as current spending, and not as investment spending, aimed at producing future benefit. As a result, the long-term benefits of spending on public services are rarely taken into account. National accounting rules incorporate that bias, by counting spending on physical assets as investment, while spending on public services, even though it builds up 'human and social capital', is seen as current expenditure. This results in infrastructure spending being biased towards physical infrastructure. This matters in terms of public discourse, but matters even more when enshrined in fiscal rules that allow borrowing only for investment (including the Labour Party's proposed fiscal credibility rule – see Part One, Policy idea 3).

For example, after years of failure to invest, our care system is now widely recognised as being in crisis. Massive investment in our care infrastructure is urgently needed – not just to help the 1.3 million people not getting the care they need, but also to transform the way that care is delivered. The initial costs of setting up a National Care Service (see 'What's the best way of delivering social care?', Part Five, Policy idea 4) would undoubtedly be high, since they would have to make up for decades of underfunding. However, these costs would reduce in the long run, since care needs would fall with better preventative investment.

Even in the short term, however, there are employment gains that would help reduce costs by raising tax revenues. The Women's Budget Group, in *Investing in the Care Economy: Stimulating Employment Affects by Gender in Countries in Emerging*

*Economies* (WBG, 2017) simulated the gains of investing in care and compared them with those of investing in construction (the typical focus of a physical infrastructure programme, funded via the capital account) across several OECD (Organisation for Economic Co-operation and Development) economies. The simulations took into account the direct and indirect employment generated in the industries in which the investment takes place and in industries supplying them, as well as the induced employment produced by the additional spending of the directly and indirectly employed workers. It was found that twice as many jobs overall would be created in the UK by investing in care than in construction. The initial simulation assumed care workers were paid at current very low wage rates; however, later simulations show that investing in care remains a better generator of employment than investing in construction, even when care workers are not poorly paid.

Another benefit of investing in social infrastructure is that much of the direct employment it generates is likely to be taken up by women (at least until higher wages and changing gender norms make such employment more attractive to men). This is in complete contrast to the employment produced by investing in physical infrastructure, since jobs in construction are almost entirely filled by men. To be consistent with equality policies, investment in physical infrastructure would therefore require mitigating measures to counteract its adverse effect on the gender employment gap (see Part One, Policy idea 3). The much greater employment generated by investment in care also means that, even though more jobs would be generated for women than men (reducing the gender employment gap), it would still create almost as many jobs for men as investing in construction.

Finally, investment in care also increases the labour force, by enabling many of those currently providing unpaid care to increase their level of employment. Thus, even in times of near-full employment, investment in care expands the economy, substantially reducing its net cost through the revenues raised from taxes paid by the newly employed and the reduced need for spending on means-tested benefits. (For an example of how net costs are reduced in this way, see Part Five, Policy idea 6.)

## What can we do?

- **Investing in social infrastructure has benefits on several timescales. In the short term, it is an effective economic stimulus that generates substantial numbers of jobs** In doing so, it decreases gender inequalities by providing employment opportunities for women, reducing their unpaid work. This would be true even if care workers were better paid, and, when there's full employment, would largely pay for itself through increased government revenues.
- **In the medium term, such a large investment should raise (women's) wages and working conditions in public services**, particularly in the care sector, where it is already difficult to recruit workers on current low pay and conditions. This will narrow the gender pay gap and should help break down gender segregation in the public sector; this will help reduce gender divisions across the economy.
- **In the long run, investment in social infrastructure will help produce high-quality public services and better outcomes for the citizens.** It should also contribute to an order less dependent on unpaid care and gender divisions in both paid and unpaid work.

# POLICY IDEA 7

# Why should the railway be renationalised?

*Jeff Tan*

## What's the issue?

Privatising railways has failed to deliver the promised better value, capital investment or reductions in public subsidies. However, successive reforms have neither renationalised the rail network nor addressed the problem of financing infrastructure – even with broad public support for change.

> **What's the case for railway renationalisation? And how should it be financed?**

## Analysis

Rail privatisation has failed on two levels. One is the well-known problem of higher costs, fares, public subsidies and grants. The other is the refusal of successive reforms to consider solutions outside the private sector to solve the problem. Much of the argument for continuing the status quo is the assumption that any failure was due to poor implementation, such as excessive fragmentation, the separation of infrastructure from operations, the rushed implementation of the franchise system and regulatory failure.

A better explanation is that privatisation is highly political. The type of privatisation that reversed over 150 years of railway consolidation was driven by political ideology and maintained by vested interests. Successive rail reforms had similar motivation, keeping the fragmented rail system in place. Vested interests include train operating companies (TOCs), rolling stock companies (ROSCOs) and thousands of railway maintenance and infrastructure companies in the subcontracting chain, all of which rely on and help justify the existing structure – for private gain.

Successive governments have also supported the privatised system. Not only have they failed to prioritise capital funding for rail and public transport, but the actual cost of railway infrastructure has also been hidden by keeping it off the government's balance sheet – first, through subsidies to TOCs to pay for track access charges, and then, through increased borrowing by Network Rail to compensate for reduced track access charges. The result has been a vast increase in Network Rail's debt – from £6.3 billion in 2002, to £46.3 billion in 2016 – with £1.7 billion in interest payments alone.

The case for rail renationalisation therefore includes savings from reintegration, as well as improved performance monitoring and more efficient financing of infrastructure.

### Savings from reintegration

The extra costs of privatised rail are the result of the forced introduction of competition – which increased costs through fragmentation and profit extraction by the private sector. Savings from reversing this, as well as eliminating both duplication (in terms of administration, management, marketing and franchise bidding) and dividend payments were estimated by the Trades Union Congress (TUC) to be £80 million per year in 2015/16, increasing to £600 million per year by 2019/20.

*Improved monitoring*

Currently, regulation is meant to ensure that efficiency gains are made and performance and investment targets are met, particularly as operating subsidies and capital grants weaken private incentives. However, regulators rarely have full access to company information, hampering their effectiveness. Their job is made harder still by a fragmented rail network, with an unnecessarily complicated regulatory environment. Renationalisation offers much simpler and better regulation, plus easier access to information for effective monitoring.

*Financing infrastructure*

Given the gulf between infrastructure costs (especially after decades of underinvestment) and socially acceptable fares, railways cannot be self-funding – and Britain already has the highest fares in Europe. Instead, financing must be linked to the wider benefits of reducing road congestion, pollution and carbon emissions, while improving social access and economic mobility. These society-wide benefits should override business models based on simple cost recovery and profitability, if rail is to be properly funded.

## What can we do?

Rail renationalisation needs to address both industry fragmentation and the funding of rail infrastructure. The underlying principles should therefore centre on network reintegration and the public financing of infrastructure, based on the society-wide benefits of rail travel. There are three key considerations:

- **Renationalise TOCs and ROSCOs.** The elimination of train operating franchises, ROSCOs and the subcontracting chain is fundamental. This could be done by:
    - not renewing TOC franchises when these expire;
    - replacing private ROSCOs with a public ROSCO or bringing the function into Network Rail;

- bringing all Network Rail's engineering and maintenance work in house;
- vertically integrating Network Rail's supply chain.

- **Rail infrastructure financing.** Proper, transparent public funding should be based on:
    - linking funding for capital investment to wider society-wide benefits, such as lower road congestion, pollution and economic regeneration;
    - separating operational costs from capital costs;
    - strictly monitoring operational costs for performance and efficiency gains;
    - keeping public capital investment firmly on the government's balance sheet, eliminating borrowing, normalising capital expenditure and making it transparent.

- **Institutional coordination and alignment.** The wider social and environmental benefits of the railway will depend on:
    - having an integrated transport policy, with rail and environmental sustainability at its core;
    - aligning government priorities through joined-up thinking, and cutting across ministries, departments and agencies to implement a transport policy;
    - developing commercial opportunities from railway assets (stations, property, land) to help finance capital expenditure.

# POLICY IDEA 8

# How can we fix the broken energy sector?

*Hulya Dagdeviren*

**What's the issue?**

In theory, the privatisation and deregulation of the UK energy sector was supposed to result in lower prices, as well as a better service for users, as a result of increased competition. But from the very beginning in the 1990s, attempts to redesign the energy market to make it live up to is promises have met with varying degrees of failure.

Energy prices did indeed decline initially, but that was mostly down to falling gas prices. Prices soon went up again – a trend that continues today. During election campaigns since, both main political parties have referred to the energy market as 'broken', proposing various ideas about how to fix it. Since free markets are not supposed to need fixing, this was embarrassing news for those supporting them – especially as similar problems were all too clear in the housing and financial markets as well. The 'Big Six' energy companies have maintained their domination, but not their customer satisfaction levels.

Overall, the energy market has clearly failed: users have often been overcharged, and security of supply remains a problem.

Clean and renewable energy has certainly grown, but this is because of government support, not as a result of competition. On the whole, it is therefore hardly surprising that opinion polls show that a large majority of the public support renationalisation.

> **What is the appropriate policy for reforming the UK energy sector?**

## Analysis

In its 2017 manifesto, the Labour Party promised to bring energy back under public control by means of a phased approach. However, the transition phase would present a number of challenges.

Some have suggested taking over some of the existing plant and supply systems of the Big Six companies, although, at least in the medium term, this would be problematic. The financial cost of renationalisation would be considerable, and in more than a few cases it would also involve buying out-of-date facilities. So, aside from considering which facilities might be bought – with water supply probably topping the list – thought should also be given to the possibility of investing in new facilities instead, ideally with the latest clean technology.

There is also a pressing need to expand capacity, especially base load supply, which supports the idea of more public sector investment. Expansion is necessary because of the scheduled retirement of major power stations over the next 10 years. The problems of the planned Hinkley Point C nuclear plant have demonstrated that the energy market is no more reliable when it comes to infrastructure investment than it is in delivering value to customers. The project has been stalled without major government guarantees and subsidies, but the choice of nuclear generation remains questionable, at best.

Public policy should clearly be aimed at new capacity creation, rather than taking over existing, outdated and overvalued facilities. Smaller, more local power suppliers (such as Robin Hood Energy, for example) could also be encouraged through incentives by local authorities, helping to diversify supply. Where more capacity is needed, it may even be necessary to prioritise these.

Diversification of suppliers could eventually put downward pressure on energy prices, but the effect will be limited during the transition phase, because getting sufficient public control of power generation will take time. Meanwhile, prices should be regulated in both retail and wholesale markets to curb the market power of the Big Six suppliers.

The ability to regulate prices should also be improved. At the moment, there are serious problems with access to the energy companies' cost data. This lack of transparent financial reporting was even highlighted by the Competition and Markets Authority in its recent investigation. Effective regulation is also hindered by the current rules on the disclosure and commercial sensitivity of data. Significant public sector involvement in the energy market at various scales of operation and with different generation technologies would provide a far better understanding of the sector, and therefore how to more effectively regulate prices.

Regulation should cover all providers – public, private, local authority and other suppliers. The current emphasis on 'competition at whatever cost' must instead give way to values that prioritise affordability, environmental goals and security of supply.

## What can we do?

- **Expansion of public sector providers in the energy market, together with price regulation**, will reduce the market power of private producers and reduce average energy prices.
- Ongoing difficulties with investment and capacity must be addressed by **effective public management**. This offers a far more integrated approach than the government's current attempts to entice the private sector to take up the incentives, subsidies and guarantees on offer. Rather, direct public investment should be planned and carried out in line with policy objectives, projections of demand growth and the planned retirement of existing plants and networks.

- Public control of the energy sector will also allow **integration with other policy areas, particularly with regard to environmental, technological development and employment strategies**.

# Interlude: Why should citizens invest in losses, rather than for profit?

## Sue Konzelmann and Marc Fovargue-Davies

As a result of the 2008 financial crisis, taxpayers bailed out the UK banks and financial institutions that caused the trouble in the first place. Not only are we unlikely to see all of that money back, which should have been invested in real services, such as the NHS; we have also been made to endure nearly a decade of austerity as a result of that 'investment', degrading public services still further. In effect, we paid for the 2008 crisis twice.

Worse still, the 2008 financial crisis is very unlikely to be the last. Aside from the few decades following the Second World War – when we had international financial regulation – financial crises have usually come along every decade or so, which means that if we don't start to do things differently, the financial sector may well be tapping us up again before much longer. That certainly suggests that, at the very least, we need a system where bailouts are repayable, so that finance doesn't get all the profits while the rest of us just get saddled with paying for the losses. Ideally, of course, strong international regulation should instead vastly reduce the scope for these crises.

This depressing story, however, can be turned on its head. Obviously, if UK citizens can be forced to 'invest' billions in failing banks for, at best, no profit, then clearly we would be able to invest in other things instead – things that actually do make a profit – which can then be used to improve the public services we want and value.

Unlike many countries, at present the UK doesn't have a sovereign wealth fund. These are usually funded by exports of commodities, such as, in the case of Norway, oil. Finance, of course, is one of the UK's main exports, and would therefore be an obvious source of funding for at least part of an investment fund for the many.

This does, of course, raise the question of who decides how and when to spend some of the proceeds of this 'citizens' wealth fund'. Obviously, deciding how to spend extra money is a far more pleasant problem than trying to work out who picks up an unexpected bill – but it's still a problem. Funding could be allocated on the basis of greatest need, although that's always going to be next to impossible to figure out; it could also be done on the basis of region, most likely by a vote.

Whatever the method, it's essential that citizens get to decide how it's spent, rather than leaving those decisions to politicians. We're constantly being told how much things cost, rather than how they should actually be done. So making some decisions ourselves would help to redress the balance.

If all of us were able to start investing like this, it might even add a new word to the financial dictionary that we can all clearly understand – 'wedge fund', perhaps?

# Part Three: Making finance work for society

## Introduction

*Sue Konzelmann and Marc Fovargue-Davies*

There are probably few people in Europe, let alone the UK, who aren't fed up with the fall-out from the 2008 financial crisis, the misery of recession and the austerity that's followed the crisis. However, if one of the aims of future policy is to reduce the number – not to mention the size – of these destructive busts, it's essential to understand what drives them.

Not enough people today remember, that for about three and a half decades following the Second World War there were virtually no financial crises; this was also a period when government policies were aimed at full employment and stable prices. The result was steadily falling public debt, rapidly rising living standards and improvements in income and wealth equality, leading some to call it the 'golden age' of capitalism.

That's odd, because since the 1970s living standards for the majority have stagnated, inequality has risen sharply and a major financial crash has come along about every decade – and, yes, that does suggest that the next one might not be too far off. So why was finance once so stable? And what caused the return of financial crises?

Like today, after the Great Depression and Second World War, many countries had also had quite enough of tough economic and social times. Financial crises – of which the 1929 Wall Street Crash that triggered the Great Depression was then merely the latest – had been a feature of capitalism since the Industrial Revolution, and many thought that they were an unavoidable part of capitalism.

However, the new post-war 'Bretton Woods' system of international financial regulation, together with tightly regulated domestic financial systems, resulted in 30 years without a crisis, where previous experience would have predicted at least three (and probably four) during that time. National financial systems and institutions were tightly regulated, the supply of credit was limited, and international capital flows were restricted. Major currencies were pegged to the US dollar, which itself was backed by gold – so exchange rates were essentially fixed. This both limited the funds available to inflate housing and stock market bubbles, and drastically reduced opportunities for currency speculation. The result was an international system that regulated both trade and – crucially – finance.

Speculation was far more difficult, and instead – as the directors of the Fidelity Fiduciary Bank in the 1964 film *Mary Poppins* put it – "You see, Michael, you'll be part of railways through Africa, dams across the Nile, fleets of ocean greyhounds, majestic self-amortising canals. Plantations of ripening tea, all from tuppence prudently, fruitfully, frugally invested...." In other words, there was not a collateralised debt obligation (CDO) in sight, and money went into real productive assets instead.

With tighter regulation, money found its way into the productive side of the economy, instead, helping to rebuild industry – much of which had been destroyed by war. This generated well-paid and secure employment for the many, helping to rebuild economies and get societies back on their feet again.

How, then, did this more successful and productive system disappear? Unfortunately, financial regulation wasn't popular with finance, and a number of developments contributed to its 'liberalisation'.

One major factor was US President Nixon's devaluation of the US dollar in 1971. This effectively wiped out the Bretton Woods fixed exchange rate system, removed restrictions on international capital flows, and fuelled inflation in worldwide commodity prices. This was made much worse by the OPEC oil price shock in 1973, in part a response to the fact that, since oil was priced in dollars, the dollar depreciation caused a sharp fall in oil producers' real income. The substantial oil price increases of 1973–74 largely returned OPEC oil prices (and corresponding revenues) to their pre-1971 levels.

In the UK, the 1970s inflation was blamed on trade union wage demands. But that meant looking at the problem the wrong way round. In reality, price inflation was driving wage claims, as unions tried to negotiate wage agreements that kept up with the rising costs of living, rather than wages driving prices.

The other key factor was that the financial sector had already found ways of getting around the post-war financial regulation. Not only had it been trading US dollars in entirely unregulated 'euro-dollar' markets since the 1950s – leading to the first major banking crisis since the war (the 1973 Secondary Banking crisis) – it was also now driving 'deindustrialisation' through corporate raiding and hostile takeovers, instead of building new businesses. The deregulated capital flows allowed speculators to buy out companies traded on the stock market – and then to asset strip them to pay back the debt used to finance the takeover. One of the effects of these buyouts was a brief spike in share prices, which was enough to convince governments that the process was having a positive effect on industrial performance; and, although the boost was very short-lived, it was enough to convince many that 'free market' activity was a good thing for the economy. However, British manufacturing industry never really recovered.

During the 1980s, with the election of Margaret Thatcher in the UK and Ronald Reagan in the US, finance moved sharply towards the 'Let's go fly a kite' model of banking. Since that time, markets – especially financial markets – have been further deregulated and liberalised. Policy shifted – away from maintaining full employment and stable prices. Employment was increasingly left to market forces, and governments focused on controlling inflation – except, of course, asset price inflation. This resulted in the return of asset bubbles and financial crises (usually followed by unhelpful austerity). Another result was acceleration of the destruction of much of Britain's productive industry, which is why we now need an ambitious industrial strategy to build new industries – and a retasked financial sector to fund it.

What does 'getting finance to work for society' actually mean? Obviously, more and better jobs benefit everyone. Apart from more people having more money to build a life, the government gets extra tax income – to help fund some of the other policy ideas outlined in this book.

The good news doesn't stop there, either. If more funds can be channelled to productive businesses – rather than inflating speculative asset bubbles – the UK's export performance can also be improved. But rather than simply aiming at a balanced budget, as recent governments have done, much improved public finances could instead help fund more programmes designed to improve the quality of life for the majority of UK citizens.

The aims, then, are clear and worthwhile. Making it happen, however, doesn't mean simply turning back the clock and reinstating the post-war system. That system was born out of the misery caused by the Great Depression, the Second World War and the Cold War, when getting coordinated international policy agreement was far easier than it is now. We are now dealing with a very different – and far more globalised – environment, where international corporations seem to wield at least as much power as some governments. This might sound a bit depressing, but the message is clear: rather than focusing on how those positive post-war outcomes were achieved, it's far better to look at what we want now, and how we might go about achieving it, given the political and financial environment we're currently in.

The policy ideas in this part of the book consider changes that would certainly have a transformative effect on the economy – and by extension, society as well – and they are all well within the scope of the UK government to implement. These ideas include ways of positively influencing corporate – especially financial sector – behaviour, through changes in both the corporate governance framework and the rules regarding limited liability. Simon Deakin develops the idea of a new Companies Act; Colin Haslam proposes reform of limited liability; and Alan Shipman develops ideas about stock market reform.

There is also the question of the kind of businesses we need – and how getting the balance right will help to support key policies elsewhere. Thus, Stewart Lansley considers how citizens' wealth funds can be used to address the problem of inequality, before Alan Shipman explores the ways that finance might be made to better serve the real economy and society. The policy ideas developed by John Marlow, Stephany Griffith-Jones and Natalya Naqvi then examine the question of how best to channel funds to start-ups and growing businesses – as well as what might be learned from other countries, such as Germany, which are already doing that very well.

## Policy ideas

1. Why the UK needs a much better Companies Act
   *Simon Deakin*
2. What should be the limits to limited liability?
   *Colin Haslam*
3. Why do we need publicly listed companies?
   *Alan Shipman*
4. How can citizens' wealth funds address the problem of inequality? *Stewart Lansley*
5. How can finance better serve the real economy?
   *Alan Shipman*
6. How can we channel credit to small and medium-sized enterprises (SMEs)? *John Marlow*
7. What can we learn from Germany's national development bank? *Stephany Griffith-Jones and Natalya Naqvi*

# POLICY IDEA 1

# Why the UK needs a much better Companies Act

*Simon Deakin*

## What's the issue?

Corporate governance is the system through which productive assets are owned, controlled and managed. At the moment, those who manage assets in the corporate sector will be accountable to shareholders, rather than workers, customers or citizens. Most of the UK economy is run like this because, since the 1980s, many state assets have been privatised, and organisations like mutual societies – responsible for the vast majority of home loans – have also been transferred to shareholder control.

This expansion of the corporate sector brought a strengthening of the rights (and therefore the potential influence) of shareholders, through changes to both company law and the 'soft law' codes governing things such as board membership, shareholder 'stewardship' (a euphemism for investor control) and takeover bids. This has undermined the interests of other stakeholders – like employees and UK citizens, generally.

Why does the UK need a much better Companies Act?

## Analysis

The shifting of control to shareholders effectively empowered collective capital, in the form of pension funds, hedge funds and sovereign wealth funds.

UK pension funds are financed by contributions from workers and employers; they are subsidised by the state, which also provides some protection to members, in the event of insolvency. Partly because of regulation and partly because of the need for stable returns over the long term, pension funds are usually relatively risk-averse in their investments.

Hedge funds, on the other hand, look for high returns over shorter periods of time, but through higher-risk activities, like arbitrage-based trading. Some specialise in pressuring the boards of cash-rich firms to 'unlock' capital by selling assets, with the proceeds being used for dividends and share buybacks. They mostly represent wealthy individuals and families.

Sovereign wealth funds represent the interests of national governments and ultimately, to some extent, their citizens. Like pension funds, they can take a longer-term view, but they are less restricted by prudential regulation and can respond to market opportunities. The proportion of the returns that gets used for public benefits, like infrastructure, or lower taxes, varies from country to country.

*Are shareholders now too powerful?*

In the late 1980s, UK-listed companies were mostly (around 80 per cent) owned by British pension funds, following the privatisation of state assets. At that point, it could have been argued (fairly convincingly) that making managers more accountable to shareholders would also be in the interests of the members of occupational pension schemes. However, the share of UK equities held by British-based pension funds has now shrunk to less than half, with overseas owners and hedge funds accounting for the rest. This makes it much harder to see how the pro-shareholder view of UK company law and corporate governance might also benefit the UK population (especially as the UK has no sovereign wealth fund).

This isn't the only reason to doubt that pro-shareholder corporate governance serves the national interest. Even at their peak, pension funds represented less than half the UK workforce, and this proportion has since dropped dramatically. Aside from a minority of British workers in defined benefits schemes, membership of a pension scheme no longer guarantees financial security.

Pro-shareholder corporate governance harms citizens in other ways, too. When a listed company opts for a dividend or share buyback, due to pressure from a hedge fund or the threat of a hostile takeover, gains to shareholders result in losses for workers (through job cuts, lower wages and more precarious work), customers (because of reduced services) and the state (through lower tax revenues).

Those in favour of shareholder empowerment have tried to argue that these investor-led losses are necessary for the longer-term health of the economy, particularly with respect to technological innovation. However, this has been largely debunked by studies that show that it's actually the state that drives innovation, through its long-term support for R&D (research and development). Today's digital technologies, for example, would not exist without long-term US government funding for the advances underpinning them. However, research fails to support the idea that increasing shareholder protection leads to more innovation; it usually has the opposite effect, by diverting corporate profits away from productive investment.

### Other problems with UK company law

Current UK company law can also actively encourage tax avoidance and regulatory arbitrage (choosing the least challenging regulatory system). The recent case of BHS is just one example of a sustainable business being hollowed out for personal gain. Most people would be amazed that burdening a company with the debt used to buy it, diverting its assets into dividends that end up in a tax haven, and then leaving the business to fail – along with its pension scheme – is apparently legal. No one responsible for the BHS debacle has yet been held to account, but this not a one-off problem; the incompetence and lack of basic skills of the business leaders behind the failure of some of the UK's largest banks following the financial crisis of 2007–08 are also apparently immune from legal accountability.

Although the problems with the UK's dysfunctional corporate governance system are becoming too obvious to ignore, it is still claimed that there is nothing that can be realistically done about them. However, although finance in the UK has long dominated productive industry, and the City of London is too powerful to be easily confronted, many of the problems we've considered are actually the result of quite recent laws.

With the adoption of the City Code on Takeovers and Mergers in the 1960s, the government began to defer to the City when designing the rules governing the productive sector. This trend continued with the Cadbury Code (later the Corporate Governance Code) in the early 1990s and the Stewardship Code in the 2000s. These all took the principle of shareholder primacy for granted. Even the hugely complex Companies Act enacted in 2006 did nothing to change this, and the few changes it did make – such as the law on directors' duties – were largely cosmetic.

## What can we do?

We need **a new Companies Act** – to take back control from the financial interests that are both making and administering corporate governance in their own interests.

A Companies Act that's fit for purpose should also do the following things:

- It should **qualify shareholder voting rights over change of control transactions** – including takeovers.
- It should **guarantee worker representation in managerial decision-making** – especially at board level.
- It must **address the use of shell companies and holding structures that facilitate tax avoidance**.
- It should **control excessive dividends, and make share buybacks illegal** again.
- It should **promote more diversity of corporate forms** (not just shareholder ownership) by encouraging worker and customer control of social enterprises.

- Finally, it should **make it easier to return assets to the state**, particularly in industries where collective ownership would be in the public interest.

# POLICY IDEA 2

# What should be the limits to limited liability?

*Colin Haslam*

**What's the issue?**

Limited liability has become a shield employed to protect value extraction and to justify behaviour that undermines the ability of UK companies to absorb financial risk, and this now presents a major moral hazard for society.

> **How should limited liability be reformed, to prevent abuse?**

**Analysis**

The mid-19th-century reform of limited liability and company law conferred privileges on shareholder-investors that encouraged them to invest in projects that were financially high risk but socially beneficial. Shareholder liability was limited to their unpaid share capital, in return for which shareholders forfeited claims to outright company ownership. Each company was granted a separate legal identity with an overriding obligation to itself, including all of its other stakeholders.

But things have moved on a great deal during the century and a half since. Instead of investing in railways and other public infrastructure, the rise of financial engineering by investment banks, private equity and hedge funds has generated not only lucrative transaction fees, but also increased capital gains for shareholders. Companies now move funds around a complex network of tiered wholly owned subsidiaries to financially engineer returns on capital for shareholders.

In terms of regulatory governance, the UK government has delegated oversight of financial reporting and standard setting to the International Accounting Standards Board (IASB), whose remit is no longer confined to public limited companies, but is spilling over into other spheres of the economy, including small and medium-sized enterprises (SMEs) and the public sector (both central and local government enterprise accounts). The IASB's agenda has been framed by two central concepts: (1) that general purpose financial statements should present a 'reporting entity's' financials; and (2) that the information disclosed by reporting entities should be 'decision useful' to investor-shareholders.

The economist's notion of the firm as a 'unit of account' has thus long since been abandoned by accountants who now use the IASB's concept of a 'reporting entity' – a company that can consolidate the financial activity of many firms. A parent company can also benefit, in its own right, from limited liability, as well as insulating itself from financial risks in wholly or partially owned subsidiaries. This is because these subsidiaries can claim limited liability if they become insolvent.

A key objective of general purpose financial reporting is to provide financial information that is useful to existing and potential investors, lenders and creditors. In this context, the shift from historical cost accounting (HCA) to fair value accounting (FVA) has been justified because it generates value-relevant information for investor-shareholders. However, many companies are depleting reserves because they pay out very high dividends and fund share buybacks. This is not only eroding the financial capacity of companies to absorb losses; it could also, like the banking crisis, put UK economic stability at risk.

## What can we do?

The institutions regulating financial reporting should be reorganised into a new institution that reinstates the 'social licence' of limited liability.

- **Companies are key actors and institutions.** The objective of policy should be to restrict corporate opportunism and rebalance corporate governance towards the public interest. Limited liability was not intended to create opportunism in companies for excessive shareholder gain.
- **Consolidated parent–subsidiary networks should be kept as simple as possible** to promote transparency for financial reporting.
- **Restrictions should be placed on the extent to which a parent company and its subsidiaries can benefit from mutually exclusive limited liability**, which may extend to the right to limited liability.
- There should be **controls on shareholder payments that damage equity reserves**. This would need a new definition of capital maintenance, including restrictions on the pooling out of resources, dividends and share buybacks if the assets/liabilities ratio falls below original and additional paid-in capital.
- **Limits should be set on the types of asset classes that can be adjusted to a 'fair' value.**

# POLICY IDEA 3

# Why do we need publicly listed companies?

*Alan Shipman*

**What's the issue?**

The stock market's short-term boom is, to a large extent, concealing its long-term shrinkage; the rising price of shares is to no small degree the result of the decreasing quantity of available shares. This is because the numbers of quoted companies and share issues have been declining, as publicly listed 'PLCs' disappear due to mergers and acquisitions, share buybacks and/or private equity-financed buyouts.

This decline in one of liberal capitalism's major institutions might seem like good news to many on the political left. But it's not quite that simple, and there are several ways that most citizens risk losing out as a result. The reprivatisation of public corporations ends any prospect of Britain developing 'democratic' ownership, where pension and insurance funds (or a sovereign wealth fund, if the UK were to set one up) hold equity and collect dividends on behalf of most UK households. Progress towards using shareholder power to improve corporate governance is socially pointless if most UK companies cease to be answerable to shareholders. Now that the door to generalised stakes in corporate ownership and profit has been firmly shut, there is a strong case for policies to reopen it.

## Why do we need publicly listed companies?

### Analysis

Stock markets have long been accused of not only prioritising short-term profit over long-term reinvestment, but also of promoting unproductive speculation and distracting investors from raising new capital by endlessly retrading the old. More recently, high frequency and algorithmic trading have raised the spectre of ever-greater volatility, and of professionals with fast programmes (or insider knowledge) beating ordinary investors to every possible capital gain. However, the drift of corporate ownership away from public stock markets might actually be even worse for labour.

The case for promoting more UK company shares on UK public stock markets – and enabling more of those shares to be owned by UK-based funds and individuals – has a number of different strands:

- Investment and pension funds have traditionally relied on listed equities to inflation-proof and build long-term savings, by capturing some of the capital gains and dividend streams that would otherwise flow to already-rich capital owners.
- New equity promotes business growth and hence employment, by providing entrepreneurs with the funds to finance expansion under professional management, without excessive borrowing.
- Public listing means accountability and information disclosure, valuable to employees and the community; not listing, or de-listing, removes this.
- Stock markets make equity stakes accessible to a broad range of investors – including collectively investing employees and the state.

- Stock markets, with a broad enough investor base, usually value large companies more reliably and improve resource allocation.
- Shareholders, especially when they hold or manage large blocks of shares, have the ability to discipline management, enforcing better corporate performance.
- While stock markets may well be short-termist, private equity funds are usually even worse, resulting in brutal cost cutting and asset stripping in pursuit of a quick 'turnaround'.

## What can we do?

- While stock markets with a wider choice of shares and better regulation should be encouraged, **alternatives to publicly listed share ownership** – other than from private equity – should also be promoted. These might include a state-invested private equity fund, direct non-traded public holdings in major companies, the channelling of pension fund holdings into public infrastructure and other collective investments, and/or the expansion of state-invested long-term capital banks as an alternative source of finance for fixed investment.
- Alongside these, however, there is still a strong public interest in **re-expanding stock markets by steering companies back towards public listing**. The dis-invention of public limited companies by buybacks and buyouts – separating limited liability from public accountability – is a regressive trend that a progressive government should seek to reverse. The 'public limited company' – a social innovation that drove the first Industrial Revolution – still has a role to play in building progressive societies, and the publicly traded share is as important a financing instrument as the government bond.
- **The 'Tobin tax' on share transactions**, designed to curb unnecessary churn, enjoys wide support, despite being difficult to implement unilaterally. Problems that would need to be addressed if 'wider share ownership' is to serve as a route to democratic capitalism include the small proportion of shares that working people can expect to accumulate. At present, the lack not only of employee control over pension funds but also of pension fund managers over corporate management

must be considered, as must the risks to employees, where pension savings are mostly invested in their own company's equity. There is also the issue of pension risk being shifted from employers and government to employees, by a switch to 'defined contribution' schemes.

- The falling supply of listed equities is partly down to two decades of abnormally low borrowing costs, which encouraged companies to grow by using debt, rather than issuing shares, or to use cheap debt to buy back their own shares. But the strong possibility that borrowing costs will rise in the near future might well result in the reversal of this trend. Since 2010, due to stricter regulatory pressure, UK banks have done this already – de-leveraging by raising new equity. But many non-financial corporations have not, and will need a vibrant stock market when the time comes.

- Even if there are factors that have permanently reduced the supply of listed firms, these mostly reflect changes that go against the public interest, such as the increased scope for a few large players to dominate global markets, thereby concentrating an industry's profit base. Other trends include the increased scale (and limited liability) of private equity partnerships, enabling them to control both the ownership of even the largest firms and the rules that facilitate share buyback, with a consequent loss of public accountability.

- There are also dangers in leaving stock markets in their present condition. The shrinking and sectoral narrowing of the supply of equities makes for greater stock market volatility and puts an artificial premium on the remaining shares. It also arbitrarily assigns instant fortunes to those who are able to move in early on the rare initial 'public' offerings.

- Whether the available equity pool has been permanently reduced – or is about to rise again due to a new wave of de-leveraging – policy must prepare for a large-scale movement of shares back on to public exchanges, so that public and privately subscribed investment funds can channel enough of their share-buying power into domestic industrial renewal.

- Fundamental steps to revive stock markets and curb their worst tendencies – which would serve the interests of the majority of the population – include:

- **Changing the favourable tax and regulatory treatment of private equity funds** – especially their ability to subtract interest 'expense' from profit, and convert the remainder into lower-taxed capital gains.
- **Reassessing the extension of limited liability from publicly listed companies to private partnerships**, which has allowed private equity funds and other service sector 'partnerships' to grow so large.
- **Strengthening competition rules**, to combat oligopoly and the concentration of profit in the largest firms, or breaking them up (into two or more listed companies) where there is evidence of suppressed competition.
- **Using a financial transactions tax** to promote investment for growth, rather than short-term gains.
- **Phasing out the artificial reduction of corporate borrowing costs caused by 'quantitative easing'**, switching to 'people's quantitative easing' and spreading the benefits beyond the financial sector.
- **Reintroducing a free float into extant state-owned corporations**, and retaining one in private companies that are nationalised in the future.
- **Promoting exchange-traded funds**, which can simulate shareholder exposure in those enterprises that are removed or withheld from public listing.

# POLICY IDEA 4

## How can citizens' wealth funds address the problem of inequality?

*Stewart Lansley*

**What's the issue?**

Although the question of inequality has been moving up the political agenda, this has yet to translate into actual policy action. The UK continues to sit near the top of the global inequality league, with its deepening economic divide set to continue to widen, with grave consequences for both social and economic stability.

> Can citizens' wealth funds inject a pro-equality force into the economy?

**Analysis**

Rising inequality has been driven by two key trends: (1) the steady rise in the share of national income accruing to capital at the expense of labour; and (2) the concentration in ownership of capital and other forms of wealth. The returns from wealth (dividends, rent and interest) therefore go disproportionally to the already well-off.

The impact on inequality of the rising capital share has largely depended on the political and economic system. In the UK and the US, with their marked dominance of private capital, antipathy to collective ownership and high capital concentration, a rising capital share has translated into higher inequality. By contrast, in those countries where capital is more equally distributed, there has been a weaker, if still upward, impact on inequality.

Changing this primary source of inequality requires, among other policies, the deconcentration of capital ownership through measures that bring a more even distribution of wealth and its gains. One possibility would be to expand the role of alternative ownership forms – from partnerships to cooperatives, which distribute economic gains more equally; another would be via the increased taxation of wealth.

One of the most effective instruments for tackling inequality would be the creation of one or more citizens' wealth funds. These are collectively held financial funds, communally owned, and used for the wider benefit of society. Their creation would raise the share of national wealth that is collectively owned, which is currently about one-tenth, compared to a quarter during the post-war era.

By increasing the share of national wealth that is held in common, such funds would bring a new 'fundamental force for convergence', a potentially powerful pro-equality instrument. They could play a key role in helping to construct a 'shared capitalism', where a rising part of the gains from economic activity are pooled and shared among all citizens and, crucially, across generations.

As well as distributing the gains from growth more widely, the funds inject a longer-term perspective into economic management and bring greater equity between generations. Such funds offer a 21st-century alternative to nationalisation and privatisation, and should be a central element of any plan for radical reform, while achieving inclusive growth.

Variants of such funds already exist, with the most successful enjoying high levels of public support. There are thus clear blueprints for a UK model. The state government of Alaska has used the proceeds of oil extraction to create a Permanent Fund, which has paid a highly popular annual citizens' dividend since the early 1980s. The Norwegian sovereign wealth fund, also funded by oil, acts as an active investor. The Australian Futures Fund, with an impressive return since its launch in 2006, was funded from the sale of the country's publicly owned telecoms giant, and helps fund both disability care costs and medical research.

There are also several UK examples of socially owned funds. These include the Crown Estate, which manages the monarch's assets independently of government, and which passes annual surpluses – £304 million in 2016 – to the Treasury. There are also the Orkney and Shetland charitable trusts, funded by local oil companies.

The following are key principles of a model UK fund:

- It should embrace the common ownership of a portion of the national wealth.
- Its funding, management and goals should be fully transparent.
- It should be managed independently of government by a Board of Guardians – including democratic input, with investment based on a mix of commercial, social and ethical criteria.
- To allow the fund to grow and survive, thus meeting the goal of inter-generational equity, only part of its value (below the expected rate of return) should be distributed each year.
- In the longer term, returns would generate new revenue streams, thus expanding the options for government. They could be used to boost spending on vital infrastructure and regeneration programmes and support key areas of social spending.

The UK has already lost two opportunities to take this path: (1) a North Sea oil-based fund created during the 1980s would now be worth over £500 billion, turning the public sector net worth (total public assets minus the gross public debt) from negative to positive; and (2) instead of privatisation, the UK could have followed other countries, such as Singapore, in pooling public assets into a single, ring-fenced fund.

The potential of such funds is now beginning to be acknowledged, with support in principle from organisations such as the Royal Society of Arts (RSA) and the Institute for Public Policy Research (IPPR). But the idea could be turned into a much more substantial initiative.

## What can we do?

Although the UK has spent most of its oil revenue, **a financial fund** could still be established using other sources of income. Because they take time to build, one possibility would be to use the current, historically low, interest rates, to kick-start the fund through government bonds with 40- or 50-year terms. The returns on such a fund should exceed the cost of borrowing. There would be no immediate change in the public sector balance sheet, as the additional liability would be matched by the new asset. A similar method – the issuing of long-term fixed government loans – was used to finance the building of the new towns from the late 1940s.

Additional funding could come from:

- **The transfer of a range of existing commercial public assets** (from property and land to a number of state-owned enterprises, such as the Land Registry) into the fund.
- **One-off taxes on windfall profits**, such as those levied on banks and energy companies.
- Direct charges on rentier activity, such as mergers and acquisitions, and corporate payments for the use of personal data.
- There is also a strong case for much of the funding to come from **higher wealth taxation**. Paying the revenue into a fund with a high degree of public visibility and support might make wealth taxation more politically palatable.

One of the most radical approaches would be to create a fund through the **dilution of existing capital ownership**, paid for by an additional, modest, annual levy on share ownership, and paid in shares. James Meade, the Nobel laureate, advocated such a pro-equality measure in the 1960s. In this way, part of the privately owned stock of capital could be gradually transferred into a national fund to be used for explicit public benefit. A variant on this model was used to create the wage-earner funds implemented in Sweden during the 1980s. The fund was closed by the incoming Conservatives in 1991, by which time it had grown to be worth some 7 per cent of the economy. Unlike the Alaskan and Norwegian approaches, it failed to win the level of public buy-in necessary for sustainability, in part because the public had no direct stake. Nevertheless, the Swedish experience offers valuable lessons for how such an approach might be explored in the UK.

The Shadow Chancellor has suggested using this source of funding to give workers in large companies a small ownership stake in the companies they work for. Under this proposal, large sections of the workforce would miss out. With a wider citizens' wealth fund, however, the benefits would be distributed collectively to *all* citizens rather than to individual employees, achieving a much more even spread of capital ownership.

A recent City University study, *Remodelling Capitalism: How Social Wealth Funds Could Transform Britain*, has shown how a fund could be built over time that would become a significant part of the national economy, and sufficient to pay an annual equal citizens' dividend, as in Alaska, and eventually a basic income for all.

For the first time ever, all citizens would hold a direct and equal stake in economic success, with the fund automatically capturing a growing part of the gains from economic activity and distributing it equally through a people's dividend. A fund would promote greater inter-generational equity by ensuring that a growing share of national wealth is held in trust for all citizens across generations. Provided it is managed with transparency and at arm's length from the state, a citizens' wealth fund offers a new tool for social democracy, partial reform of corporate capitalism and a new 21st-century social contract between citizen, state and market.

# POLICY IDEA 5

# How can finance better serve the real economy?

*Alan Shipman*

## What's the issue?

Following the 2008 financial crisis, UK financial regulation was redesigned, putting much more emphasis on providers' financial soundness, as well as on monitoring systemic risk. But, although it is an improvement, the current combination of prudential, systemic and retail financial regulation is still more likely to drive excessive risk-taking out of sight (and off the balance sheet) than to reduce it. It will probably also increase moral hazard for customers, who are likely to assume that financial products and selling processes have been officially tested and approved. Nor does current regulation address the problem of 'too-big-to-fail' financial institutions counting on state aid in the event that their gambling losses prove excessive.

Equally worrying is the softening of safeguards for customers (small and large businesses, and households trying to build savings and pensions), whose value for money has been reduced by the need to rebuild providers' profits, while the safety of their money is still not guaranteed.

How can finance be made to serve the real economy and society better?

## Analysis

While their early performance has so far been good, given their limitations, the new regulatory arrangements won't be effective unless the regulation of *conduct* is matched by equally tough guidelines for financial *products* and *structures*. These were once central to regulation, resulting in fewer fraud, mismanagement and mis-selling scandals – not to mention, systemic crises. On its own, conduct-based regulation will always limit regulators' effectiveness – not least because financial firms can not only easily overwhelm even the best watchdogs with excessive detail; they can also conceal vital facts and/or blind them with alchemy. Without product and structural regulation, the UK will continue to be saddled with an over-expanded financial sector that short-changes its clients and fails to deliver the higher returns it promises to justify excessive (and ultimately socialised) risk.

Many who praise (and/or practise in) banking, insurance and securities trading firms agree that regulators will never foresee every looming crash – partly because they tend to prepare for yesterday's crisis instead of the next one. They also lack the information that would allow them to monitor whole markets for risk. And with increasingly high-speed automated trading (the social value of which is entirely unclear), regulators might well be unable to process the data in time, even if they had it.

History strongly suggests that lasting financial stability is only achieved when governments support regulation not only of financial firms' behaviour, but also their products, while setting clear, simple rules governing industry structure. This is to no small degree a consequence of conduct regulation being essentially retrospective; inappropriate conduct, such as mis-selling, needs regulation to be in place before it can be tackled. By contrast, regulation of product and structure design tends to be more future-proof, as efforts to innovate around current design rules are easier to detect than efforts to bend the rules of conduct.

This kind of regulation is entirely normal in other sectors of the economy that can significantly affect household welfare and economic health. For example, state agencies tell healthcare providers what drugs and operations they can legally provide. They require approval of building designs and check them during construction. Carmakers, meanwhile, are required to meet ever-tougher safety and emission standards, and will soon be given deadlines for discontinuing diesel and non-hybrid engines. Industry structures are also routinely monitored for signs of excessive market power, as well as conflicts of interest – especially where one firm deals on both sides of a market. It is unclear why finance should be differently treated, when there is clear evidence that the economic and social costs of product innovation and structural change after deregulation have outweighed the benefits.

Until the 1980s, the UK financial sector had a clear division between commercial and investment banking, as well as between mortgage lending (by building societies with high capital ratios) and business lending (by commercial banks). There were rules that limited the extent to which lenders borrowed funds from wholesale markets and resold packages of loans to them, which encouraged lenders to monitor borrowers and guard against default. Rules like these, if retained, would have helped regulators detect and address the systemic problems behind the 2007–08 financial crisis earlier, if not wholly averting them. They might also have discouraged the replacement of productive investment with real-estate lending, which has left the UK with over-inflated property prices and a chronically underfunded industrial sector.

Financial innovation, unlike that in the real economy, has not been convincingly linked to either economic growth or welfare improvement. In fact, the 'socially useless' nature of many of these new products is routinely criticised by commentators and regulators alike. By contrast, most socially useful financial innovations have been regulation-led: tradable bonds, publicly listed shares – as well as the limited liability attached to them – and even the European Union's (EU) globally exported UCITS (undertaking for collective investment in tradable securities) – all followed standards set down by legislation. The markets where they trade, and derivative contracts based on them, have long depended on contract enforcement by public courts, and are now just as reliant on public monitoring of systemic risk.

The case for product regulation is reinforced by the regular episodes of mis-selling, caused by the proliferation of products with minor variations in design and small-print conditions. This has been clearly shown to inhibit consumers' ability to choose, while the lack of transparency supports intermediaries, who profit by adding on commissions and other extra costs. On the consumer side, the search engines that attempt to compare these products, nudging customers towards the ones that supposed experts claim will serve their needs, or the investigation and punishing of mis-selling after it has already happened, are hardly ideal fixes. A progressive government needs to reintroduce product standards and structural rules, whose absence has proved so damaging.

## What can we do?

- Unregulated competition has clearly failed to either lower costs or raise standards in the financial sector – with some very unhelpful effects on industry, housing, families and the UK's national finances. As a result, **rethinking regulation** is essential for setting the rules. But this doesn't mean trying to turn the clock back so much as designing regulation to deal with current conditions. The rapid rise of FinTech (financial technology), unforeseen in the 1980s and 1990s when regulation was being relaxed, adds urgency to the question of how to assess new types of product and structure, and anticipate their social costs and benefits.

- Financial institutions, accustomed to extensive input into UK policy and rule design, fiercely resist most regulatory tightening. **Reinforcing structural and product regulation** in financial services will, in all likelihood, be opposed by some, on the grounds that it will downsize an industry that ranks among the country's most successful (in terms of contributions to both exports and GDP), and straitjacket one that has thrived on innovation. Its defenders might also point to a reluctance to offer legislatively specified products, such as 'stakeholder pensions' or basic bank accounts, as a sign that government intervention would make the sector uncompetitive.

- Against these objections, a progressive government must recognise that the apparent success of UK financial services is based entirely on its ability to make profits for bankers and financial traders, rather than the services it provides to household and corporate customers. Equally significant is that its profits and exports have been effectively underwritten by the public sector – which covered the losses of the 2007–08 crisis – at the cost of many public services.

- There is also the question of how much advantage we actually get from our over-expanded financial sector, even when it is – in theory at least – working properly. In terms of such things as the mark-up of borrowing costs over the base rate, investment fund expense ratios, performance of 'defined contribution' pensions, industrial and infrastructure investment rates, UK financial services customers are actually no better (and frequently worse off) than those in other countries with much smaller financial sectors. Indeed, the UK's unusually large financial service 'output' (as a share of GDP) can be seen as a clear indication of its *in*efficiency from a customer perspective, with inflated costs and higher risk encouraged by 'light touch' regulation.

- The huge cost (in both financial and social terms) of the relaxation of financial regulation has already resulted in some restructuring of industry governance. But this has not gone far enough. Regulation of finance can only hope to be effective if the sector's structure and products are simplified so that regulators can actually see what they are dealing with – and have the powers to effectively monitor and enforce the rules.

- The following guidelines for financial regulation would serve the interests of the majority of the population:
  - **Strengthen regulation of conduct, products and structures** – accepting that a 'light touch' is not enough – so that financial authorities have the ability and power to monitor and enforce the rules.
  - **Simplify financial products and structures – seeking to eliminate those that have proved**

**'socially useless'** – so that regulators can see what they are dealing with and monitor effectively.

- **Break up 'too big to fail' financial institutions**, while recognising that increased competition can drive adverse changes in corporate and individual behaviour, especially over risk-taking and mis-selling.
- **Separate both investment banking from retail and commercial banking and mortgage lending from business lending** to protect households and businesses, and ensure that finance serves its 'utility' function of serving the real economy and society.

## POLICY IDEA 6

# How can we channel credit to small and medium-sized enterprises (SMEs)?

*John Marlow*

**What's the issue?**

Labour's 2017 manifesto proposed a National Investment Bank (NIB), plus a network of regional development banks. A £250 billion 'National Transformation Fund' would focus on infrastructure and housing, while the NIB would provide £25 billion/year lending to small businesses, 'transforming our financial system' in the process. Meanwhile, the Scottish Government is looking at an NIB of its own.

The ambition is clear, but why is the current system not working? And what would a new structure have to do differently, to achieve game-changing results?

> What's the best way to channel more credit to small and medium-sized enterprises (SMEs)?

## Analysis

Several reports have proposed expanding public investment banking beyond the (now privatised) Green Investment Bank and the (still tiny) British Business Bank. Others have looked at Scotland and the now-state-owned Royal Bank of Scotland (RBS). A report to the Shadow Chancellor offered three possibilities:

- A system based on public-equity-plus-bond-issuance financing.
- Lending to commercial banks for 'on-lending' to SMEs.
- A governance structure overseen by national and regional supervisory boards with political, business and union representation.

What most public investment banks *actually* do, is to give slightly discounted loans to commercial banks, in the hope that they will, in turn, lend it to SME clients. The existing 'Funding for Lending' scheme and the Bank of England's 'Term Funding Scheme' both 'work' this way, but have not substantially boosted SME funding. The problem is that banks are not actually obliged to pass on the public money to businesses, but can instead use it to buy bonds, issue mortgages, pay dividends and so on.

One possible solution might be to demand that banks list all loans nominally issued with public money, while another might be to provide guarantees for specific SME loans. Neither, however, would show whether these loans would have been made anyway, without the public money. So it would not be possible to measure their effect.

SMEs are expensive to finance, so in theory, more could be funded were loans cheaper, longer-term or with fewer collateral requirements. In terms of scale, the proposed £25 billion/year by the NIB is significant – equivalent to around 20–25 per cent of current SME investment and all their current external financing. While increasing investment by such an amount should have significant impact, we still can't expect that cheap liquidity to translate into a £25 billion increase in SME financing, especially if commercial banks could still put the money to other uses than SME funding.

## What can we do?

The UK public banking model should be designed to tackle the obvious shortcomings of the existing financial system. Three key policies would address the main ones:

- **Target the margin.** This means putting quality over quantity, supporting businesses likely to encounter financial constraints and/or offering high social returns – such as very small firms and coops. This implies being more specific about the kinds of business being supported. Public banks, however, often do the reverse, pushing for very broad eligible investment categories. The definition of an SME is also very broad, and can include quite large firms. So without specific categories, it would be difficult to tell whether public lending has simply gone to companies that would have been funded anyway, without an SME programme.
- **Build a locally accountable public banking service.** Financial markets, especially those in Britain, don't provide the local business banking services that are essential to SMEs. One solution might be a network of local, public service-oriented banks, similar to the *Sparkassen* in Germany. Another possible model is the Banking for the Common Good proposals for a network of 'People's Banks', closely linked with local credit unions and other mutual institutions in Scotland, as is the New Economics Foundation's proposals for the future of RBS.
- **Other forms of local accountability.** Standard governance practice for state investment banks involves political oversight via a supervisory board, with operational control left to a board of appointees, typically from the banking sector. This system has roots in the 'free market' culture and is actually designed to prevent any real political involvement. So it is not always good at delivering against wider policy aims.

The proposals for local bank networks come with a different governance system, involving local government, employees and other local stakeholders, each making up one-third of the supervisory board. This should also be replicated at the national level, with the NIB accountable to national and regional governments, employees and the local bank network it would serve.

## POLICY IDEA 7

# What can we learn from Germany's national development bank?

*Stephany Griffith-Jones and Natalya Naqvi*

**What's the issue?**

The private financial system is not designed to support the real economy and, therefore, cannot support or sustain a new industrial strategy either. With an appetite for short-term, high-return speculation, it simply doesn't fund enough longer-term investment in risky innovation, neglects sectors including physical and social infrastructure, and fails to adequately support small and medium-sized enterprises (SMEs). Therefore a national investment bank (NIB) will be a valuable asset in helping to achieve more productive investment – to help the UK economy become more dynamic, greener and fairer.

> **What role could a national investment bank play in creating a better investment environment to support industrial policy?**

## Analysis

The NIB would be a strategic instrument for channelling financial resources required to deliver industrial policy, to help both rebalance the UK economy towards manufacturing and useful services, and increase dynamism and productivity.

The 2007–08 financial crisis brought renewed support for national development banks worldwide, as the problems of a purely private financial sector became more obvious. The private financial system has been pro-cyclical, over-lending in boom times but rationing credit during and after crises. It has also tended to under-fund long-term investment in the riskier innovation that many firms need to not only grow but also create high productivity jobs in the process. Funding for key sectors, such as infrastructure (physical and social), has also been neglected. SMEs – especially start-ups – often have difficulty in accessing credit, which is usually both costly and short-term. The implication is clear: delivering enough finance, at the right price, to achieve economic and social policy objectives, requires public banking institutions.

National development banks have long been an important feature of most developed as well as emerging economies – especially the most successful ones such as Germany, China, India, South Korea and Japan. The UK is an exception, having no such bank, despite its evident need. Both private and public investment have been historically low in the UK economy, falling further since the 2007–08 crisis, not least as a result of misguided austerity policies. The UK remains in last place among both the G7 and OECD (Organisation for Economic Co-operation and Development) countries, with the lowest share of investment in GDP.

One vital element in facilitating a development bank's ability to make a significant contribution to industrial policy and structural transformation is adequate scale. Germany's KfW is probably the most successful and effective national development bank in Europe. It is therefore unsurprising that Germany is the most dynamic and diversified European economy. With assets of over €500 billion, KfW is also one of the world's largest development banks as a percentage of GDP – and one of Germany's largest banks of any sort.

KfW approves new loans of around €50–55 billion each year, for domestic purposes. As the population of the UK is around 80 per cent of Germany's, a comparable lending capacity for the UK would be around €42 billion (£37 billion) per annum. The total exposure of KfW is around €500 billion (£440 billion); again, assuming a similar scale for the UK, in proportion to its population, total exposure of the NIB should eventually reach about £350 billion.

Achieving this loan volume, assuming a leverage ratio of 1:9 (to help achieve an AAA rating), the NIB would require equity of £40 billion, consisting mainly of public paid-in capital. However, if profits are generated, these could be reinvested into the bank, allowing it to expand lending volume, without further public capital. This is what happens with banks like KfW, or the European Investment Bank (EIB). Funding high volumes of loans quickly, however, will require significant capital upfront – for example, £10 billion a year, for four years.

The German government guarantees to KfW meant that it was able – even during the financial crisis and after some losses – to keep its AAA rating, with equity of €11.7 billion, by comparison to the €37 billion likely to have been required without such guarantees. So the potential amount of capital for a British NIB could be significantly reduced – perhaps eventually by as much as a half or one-third – when the new institution has gained the confidence of bond investors.

Even though KfW loans have a general government guarantee, they don't count towards the 3 per cent public deficit-to-GDP ratio Maastricht target, according to European statistical conventions. There is therefore a strong argument that future British NIB loans should not be included in the government deficit target or in government debt. The logic is that these loans will promote growth, and hence reduce, rather than increase, the future debt-to-GDP ratio.

It is important to stress that, although the UK NIB would be publicly owned (the government providing the initial capital), it could still fund its operations in the private capital markets, as well as co-finance its operations with private lenders and investors, and most of its funds would be on-lent by private banks.

This shows that, like the German KfW and other development banks, the UK NIB's relationship with the private financial and non-financial business sector would be one of collaboration rather than competition. This has the virtue of leverage, as, with relatively scarce public resources committed as paid-in capital, it could catalyse lending and investment on a far larger scale than its public resources contribution. This leverage is vital for a government committed to structural transformation – which requires significant investment.

NIBs can also work with each other. European Union (EU) member states, for example, have widened the remit of their national development banks, but especially that of the EIB, which saw its capital doubled in 2012. Its role was expanded under the Juncker Plan, to provide up to €500 billion of additional loans between 2015 and 2020. To do that, the EIB would collaborate with the national development banks.

## What can we do?

- The NIB will be a valuable strategic instrument for government to help achieve **increased investment in the UK's real and social economy**, making it more dynamic, greener and fairer.
- International experience and the limitations of a purely financial sector – the aims of which rarely match government policy objectives – confirm the great value of such a bank for the UK.
- It is key that the NIB has **sufficient scale** to do the job.
- Funding itself in the UK and international private capital markets will allow the NIB to **leverage scarce public resources**, leading to large impact.
- The impact of the NIB could be further enhanced if the UK remains in the EIB.

## Interlude: Safe as (council) houses...

Sue Konzelmann and Marc Fovargue-Davies

There has been much talk in the media about the lack of housing in the UK. But many of us don't have to watch TV to know that there's a problem – we're living the nightmare. 'Generation Rent' is not only experiencing a shortage of housing; there's also low wages, high rents and a fair bit of badly maintained and/or low-quality accommodation to contend with.

But simply building more 'affordable' housing for sale won't solve the problem. As soon as a house enters the market, its price will inevitably rise well beyond 'affordable' levels. If a local authority in London wants to buy back an ex-council home, for example, it will face an asking price around six times what the house was originally sold for.

There's nothing inherently wrong with renting a home – after all, most of Europe still does. There are, however, significant problems in Britain's private rental market – high rents, poor maintenance and low-quality homes being among the most common complaints. However, rather than supporting more public sector housing, various attempts to control rents and improve standards have been tried, but the problems continue.

Back in the day, local authority or 'council' housing was a very different proposition to many current privately rented homes. Not only were they built solidly in the first place (bizarrely, affordable housing has its own – and stronger – set of building regs); they were also properly maintained, and local government was in full control of the rents.

Council homes, however, were among the very first victims of privatisation, with Margaret Thatcher's 'Right to Buy' scheme reducing their numbers from 6.5 million in 1980 to around 2 million in 2019 – while making it difficult for more to be built. A recent article in *The Observer*, however, based on data obtained under the Freedom of Information Act, shows that the mass sell-off has not exactly resulted in the promised 'property-owning democracy'. Instead, over 40 per cent of the council homes sold off in London are now in the hands of private landlords – with some owning up to six homes. Worse still, local authorities are now forced to spend tens of millions to fund rents that are higher than their own – on homes they used to own outright. But councils wanting to buy back those homes, so that they could offer lower rents, would, of course, have to pay far more than they originally sold them for.

All of this means that escalating private rents are a real problem for local authorities as well as tenants – especially when they're met by housing benefit payments. In some cases, UK citizens are now effectively subsidising overpriced, poor-quality accommodation with money that could be better used to fund other services – hardly the improved value for money we were led to expect from privatisation.

Feeling comfortable and secure at home is a basic building block for being able to contribute fully at work, with our families and with other people. We won't get the best out of Britain – or the best value for public money – without fixing this problem.

# Part Four:
# Genuine social security

## Introduction

*Susan Himmelweit*

After decades of neoliberal policies, growing inequality has left many of us leading increasingly insecure lives. A genuine social security system has become all the more necessary, but, instead, austerity has undermined even the minimal safety net system we once had.

Opportunities for the financial services industry have replaced social policy in this area. This has led to increases in household debt, with catastrophic consequences for some. Unregulated lending has also led to house price rises that have put proper housing beyond the reach of most young people. And we can no longer rely on the state pension to provide for our old age. Instead, we have a system that has privatised responsibility for provision in old age, relying on people saving in private and occupational pensions, helped by massive tax hand-outs to those who can afford to save most. This will leave those whose lifetime earnings are reduced by disability, discrimination or time spent out of the labour market caring for others, particularly women, in poverty in their old age.

Rather than being recognised as providing income security for all, the social security system has been recast as 'welfare' for the 'not very deserving' poor. This has enabled billions of pounds to be taken from the incomes of the poorest, until recently almost without protest, on the pretext of reducing the deficit, while at the same time income tax, the fairest tax we have, has been cut. Again, it is those whose earning capacity is most restricted who have paid the most for these policies. As the House of Commons Library has shown, by 2020 women will have paid for 86 per cent of the costs of fiscal consolidation achieved by changes in personal taxes and benefits since 2010, while men will have paid for just 14 per cent.

This policy ideas presented in this part of the book consider how some of these issues could be addressed and how the social security system could be reconstructed to become the basis of genuine social solidarity between individuals and generations. They start with innovative ideas for beginning to tackle the debt and housing crises, by Johnna Montgomerie, and Beth Stratford and Duncan McCann respectively. Then Bruno Bonizzi and Jennifer Churchill, recognising that the state pension needs to be increased if income security in old age is to be guaranteed, look at how occupational pensions could be reformed so that they provide additional income security and share risks.

The next two policy ideas examine consequences of our social security system. John Grahl argues that the UK's harsh and dysfunctional social security system is one of the main causes of mental health problems among its recipients. Simon Deakin looks over time at how successive governments have developed social security systems that have contributed to the UK's low-paid, precarious and casual labour market. They argue, respectively, for a direct focus on the wellbeing of the long-term sick and disabled, and for supportive macroeconomic and labour market policies to back up a revived social insurance system.

The last two policy ideas debate the issue of Universal Basic Income (UBI), a hotly debated potential reform in which an unconditional basic income would be paid to all citizens. Stewart Lansley and Howard Reed show how a limited scheme could be affordable, while Ian Gough rejects such a policy in favour of labour market reform and investment in public services.

## Policy ideas

1. How can we tackle the UK's private debt crisis?
   *Johnna Montgomerie*
2. How can we address the concerns of renters, without
   crashing house prices? *Beth Stratford and
   Duncan McCann*
3. How do we make occupational pension funds fit for
   purpose? *Bruno Bonizzi and Jennifer Churchill*
4. How can we stop the social security system
   aggravating mental distress? *John Grahl*
5. Reconstructing social security *Simon Deakin*
6. How could Universal Basic Income (UBI) improve
   social security? *Stewart Lansley and Howard Reed*
7. Would Universal Basic Income (UBI) address the
   causes of inequality, ill-being and injustice? *Ian Gough*

# POLICY IDEA 1

# How can we tackle the UK's private debt crisis?

*Johnna Montgomerie*

**What's the issue?**

There is growing public policy concern over the historically unprecedented level of household debt, but little by way of proposed solutions to deal with it.

> Is this level of private household debt a problem requiring action by an incoming progressive government? Can public policy address such unprecedented levels of household debt?

**Analysis**

Current high household debt levels are the result of over two decades of promoting finance-led growth, in which easy credit fuelled asset bubbles and drove consumer demand despite stagnant wage growth.

Finance-led growth refers to the shifting pattern of accumulation from productive to financial activities since the 1980s. The 2008 global finance crisis exposed the fragile balancing act required to manage finance-led growth. The basic contradiction lies in rapidly growing private debt stock and stagnating income flows.

A finance-led growth model requires private debt to generate demand that would not otherwise be there. This demand drives up property prices and fuels consumer spending through more indebtedness and persistently stagnant wage incomes.

Understanding how finance-led growth operates requires recognising that banks create money by opening debt deposit accounts when new loan contracts are issued. Efforts since the crisis to replenish capital reserves and focus on macro-prudential regulation have not changed the unrivalled commercial power of banks to create money by issuing new loans. Banks then bundle together and resell loan contracts multiple times across global financial markets. The original debt and all subsequent claims to the interest payments on that debt are wholly dependent on current incomes of households to keep up repayments. This 'originate and distribute' retail banking business model, which caused the 2008 financial crisis, remains largely unchanged.

The size and scope of household debt is an economic and societal problem, but with little recognition at public policy level.

Figure 7 shows the total stock of debt owed by the household sector, £1.545 trillion, of which 86 per cent was mortgage debt (£1.344 trillion). Public policy has promoted home ownership as a means of making households responsible for their own future needs. Households are presumed to accumulate savings in the value of their primary residence, which as they grow older provides a cash reserve at times of need and income flow for retirement. These assumptions largely ignore that residential property has become a highly leveraged form of investment because house price increases are fuelled by cheap credit.

The benefits of house price appreciation are unequally distributed across the household sector, going primarily to the older age demographics, and to homeowners living in London and the South East. As well as failing to tackle the housing crisis, this geographic and demographic concentration fuels already pronounced trends in income and wealth inequality. More problematically, the large debt now required by younger

**Figure 7:** Levels of UK household debt (1997–2018)

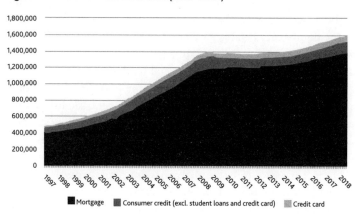

Mortgage ■ Consumer credit (excl. student loans and credit card) ■ Credit card

households to enter the housing market creates a legacy of debt for another generation to come. And not just among the young; there has been a rapid growth in home equity loans taken out by retired homeowners who are using debt to augment inadequate pensions. These are just some examples of how rising levels of debt undermine the assumption that homeownership offers an unproblematic route to prosperity and self-sufficiency that everyone can access.

According to the Bank of England, consumer debt is also at an all-time high of £201.5 billion, with credit card debt at £68.7 billion. Too often consumer debt is considered the product of profligate spending. It is more appropriately seen as the engine of consumer demand and a major profit centre for the retail banking industry. Persistently stagnant wages, especially since 2008, when a growing number of households experienced real wage decline, suggest that rising consumer debt is the dominant source of the growth in consumer demand in the UK economy. In the 12 months from March 2017 to 2018 average total debt per household, including mortgages, was £57,005, approximately 113.8 per cent of average earnings. In other words, debt levels increased by 10 per cent over these 12 months, while household incomes rose by only 1.5 per cent over the same period.

More troubling is the emerging trend of households using debt as a safety net to cope with unemployment, illness or a one-off emergency. The cost of emergency borrowing varies drastically by income and wealth: the better-off can access cheap credit by borrowing against the equity in their homes, those without home equity may be able to access lines of credit or credit cards, while the lowest-income groups pay the highest interest rates to use payday and other fringe financial lenders.

As the cost-of-living crisis becomes more pervasive, households are increasingly turning to debt simply to meet basic household cash flow needs. According to the debt charity StepChange, debt is increasingly being used to cover essential expenses such as the rent/mortgage, council tax and electricity.

Debt can also be a significant drag on growth, when households use current income to service debts rather than to spend or invest. This is the basic mechanism of a 'balance sheet recession'. Almost 10 years after the financial sector received its first bailout, most of the household sector continues to struggle to repay the stock of debt accrued during the boom years. As current income is used to service these debts, it creates a drag on economic renewal. For example, in the 12-month period from May 2018, over £50 billion, or an average of £138 million per day, was diverted in this way from potential spending or investment directly into bank revenues.

UK public policy commitments to 'austerity' compound the problem by advocating the simultaneous de-leveraging (paying down debts) of both the public and private sectors. However, rather than paying down debts, austerity has increased the overall debt stock. Large-scale cuts to government income transfers and social security, without any attempt at fiscal stimulus to promote wage growth or more stable employment, essentially shift the costs of economic recovery on to the household sector using private debt. UK economic policy is so dependent on rising private debt that the Office for Budget Responsibility (OBR) regularly predicates the UK's future growth on rising household debt level.

While households are dependent on debt to maintain living standards, the whole macro-economy is dependent on household debt to sustain aggregate demand, which feeds employment and growth. However, without wage growth, stable employment or a social safety net, the household sector's ability to sustain the ever-growing national private debt stock is precarious.

If every household struggling with debt decided to pay down their debts, the national economy would be plunged into depression. However, if households struggling with debt continue to take on more debt to maintain their standard of living, there would soon be rising insolvency rates. Currently, most households keep up their debt repayments and regularly remit a growing portion of their current income to pay for all past expenditures. If, for whatever reason, households are unable to make these regular repayments, a worse scenario would unfold in which rising default rates add to the portfolio of non-performing loans on banks' balance sheets. As the 2008 financial crisis revealed, the elaborate network of financial claims flowing through the global financial system is highly vulnerable when there is default on even small-scale household-level loans (US sub-prime mortgages). Rising default rates in the household sector would, once again, start letting off sparks that could set off another firestorm across global markets.

## What can we do?

Analysis of the scale and scope of private debt in the UK shows that it is unsustainable to rely on the household sector to fuel macroeconomic growth by taking on ever increasing levels of debt. Continuing to ignore household indebtedness as a public policy issue is reckless. Potential policies are:

- **Make cheap credit a public good.** Banks enjoy access to credit at negative real interest rates: the base rate is 0.75 per cent and inflation is 2.3 per cent. At the same time, the household sector pays for credit on a sliding scale from 2–4.5 per cent for residential mortgages, 3.5–6.5 per cent on consumer loans, 16–19 per cent on credit cards and well over 500 per cent on fringe financial products. If cheap credit is ultimately underwritten by the UK taxpayer, then credit needs to be treated as a public utility (not a private source of profit for banks) by giving the household sector access to low-cost credit already enjoyed by the banks. Lower interest rates would reduce the burden of debt on households' current income, but it would not prevent over-indebtedness.

- **The UK's residential housing market needs to be de-leveraged to become affordable, more equitable and sustainable over the long term.** After years of a credit-fuelled bubble, housing can no longer provide a reliable source of savings for homeowners, and the bubble needs to be deflated before it explodes.
- **One way of doing this would be to offer a long term refinancing operation (LTRO) for homeowners.** Put simply, debt linked to a primary residence would be able to access refinancing at a lower interest to reduce the debt burden of the large mortgages that were bid up by speculation and cheap credit during the boom years prior to 2008. This would reduce the repayment burden on household income, giving households more of their own income to spend. Refinancing a large portion of the mortgage debt stock would also begin to unwind the credit house price bubble by reducing the profitability of residential mortgage debt securities, sending investors elsewhere in search of better yields. Preventing another round of house price inflation in the residential housing markets will require a complete modernisation of existing regulation and structural reform of mortgage markets. An LTRO will lessen the pain for homeowners of weaning the economy off its dependence on residential mortgages to drive growth.
- Another way of doing this is proposed in 'How can we address the concerns of renters, without crashing house prices?' (Policy idea 2, this part of the book).
- **Household sector income growth and employment markets that generate wage gains** are necessary to abate the household sector's and public policy's dependence on debt to sustain living standards and drive economic growth. However, without debt restructuring or relief for indebted households, any income gains will be diverted directly into the financial system as such households seek to pay off their debts.
- **Developing a comprehensive strategy for household debt cancellation** offers the most direct route to ending the fragile finance-driven growth model and ending the ongoing economic crisis experienced by the household sector since 2008.

# POLICY IDEA 2

# How can we address the concerns of renters, without crashing house prices?

*Beth Stratford and Duncan McCann*

## What's the issue?

Rising house prices and rent prices systematically undermine the progressive vision of a society with equal opportunities for all. But falling house prices threaten negative equity, bank insolvencies and economic contraction. Fear of a house price crash stands in the way of bold action to tackle our housing crisis. The Common Ground Trust proposal, as published in its *Land for the Many* report to the Labour Party (Monbiot et al, 2019), offers a route out of this fix, and a mechanism for socialising the unearned land rents that are currently captured by landlords and mortgage lenders.

> How can we respond to the urgent concerns of renters and make homeownership accessible again, without pushing existing homeowners into negative equity?

## Analysis

House price inflation over the past two decades has been driven more by *expansions in effective demand* than by shortages in overall supply. First, seismic changes in the UK mortgage market – including the lifting of various restrictions on banks and building societies, the growth of securitisation and the lowering of the Bank of England base rate – have dramatically increased the supply of cheap, easy credit, and thereby boosted purchasing power available to all buyers. Second, the increasing treatment of homes as financial assets, by global and domestic elites, as well as ordinary households seeking security in retirement, has put enormous upward pressure on prices. Most significantly, buy-to-let landlords have benefited from a highly advantageous fiscal and regulatory environment in their bidding war with first-time buyers.

Fortunately, it is perfectly possible to bring these inflationary forces under control through the reforms summarised in Figure 8. Perhaps the most urgent are reforms to the private rented sector. These make sense on their own terms – since the constant threat of rent hikes and evictions is having a detrimental effect on the health and life chances of millions – but they have the added benefit of dampening demand from buy-to-let investors, and therefore removing one of the key drivers of house price inflation.

The problem is that, once house prices begin to falter, the feedbacks between mortgage lending, house prices and investor behaviour that push prices up during a boom can quickly slip into reverse. Banks become more cautious about extending mortgages, and households more cautious about taking out large mortgages. Just as demand in the housing market can be inflated by an increase in the availability of bank credit, it can be deflated by a decrease in the availability of bank credit. And, as the Bank of England has repeatedly warned, the behaviour of investors tends to amplify house price movements during a downturn, just as it does during a boom.

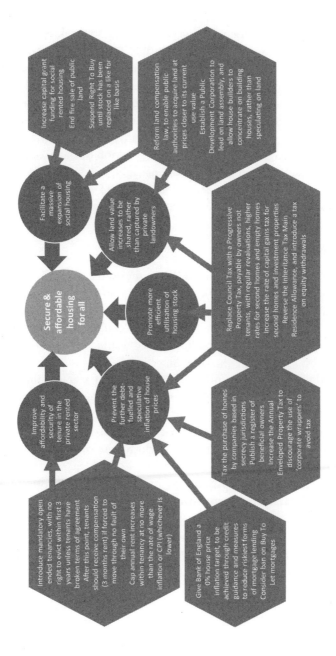

**Figure 8:** Policies to ensure affordable and secure housing for all

A fall in prices would, of course, be welcomed by many people who are currently locked out of homeownership. But falling nominal house prices also carry political, social and macroeconomic risks. A price fall could push a significant minority of households into negative equity, making it difficult to either move house or remortgage. This would be particularly problematic for those coming to the end of cheap introductory mortgage deals. Mortgage defaults could, in turn, affect the solvency of major banks, whose balance sheets are now dominated by mortgage loans. Meanwhile, households worried about their loss of housing equity may cut back on consumer spending, leading to a general contraction of the economy.

A lack of preparedness for managing these risks is a major barrier to systemic reform of our housing system. The Common Ground Trust is offered partly as a way out of this deadlock.

## What can we do?

**The Common Ground Trust** (hereafter, Trust) is proposed as a publicly backed but independent non-profit institution that would buy land from underneath houses and lease it to members.

People (including housing coops) could approach the Trust when they had found a house they wanted to buy and ask the Trust to purchase the land. Since bricks and mortar account for 30 per cent of the price of a property on average, this would allow people to put down much lower deposits and take on much lower mortgage debt than is currently the case. New buyers would sign a lease that would make them members of the Trust and entitle them to exclusive use of the land in return for paying a land rent.

The Trust is a **vehicle for bringing land gradually and voluntarily into common ownership**, with three goals in mind:

- **To expand the number of people ready and able to buy a house**, offsetting the reduction in demand from landlords and speculators. This would make it safe to improve tenants' rights, property taxation and mortgage regulation (see Figure 8), so that nominal house prices can be stabilised.

- **To reduce the scale of land rents extracted by financiers and landlords**, and to use those rents instead **to provide a safety net for members who have hit hard times**.
- **To give more people the opportunity to enjoy a form of private or mutual home ownership**. Even with improved conditions in the private rented sector, many people will have an understandable desire for a home they can substantially renovate and invest in, and the assurance that they will never receive an eviction notice.

*How would it work?*

The first step would be for the Trust to undertake a valuation of the land and the bricks and mortar. (New computational techniques and big data should make the land and property valuation process far less painstaking than it might have been in the past.) This valuation would form the basis of the Trust's offer to the prospective homebuyer:

- How much the Trust would contribute for the purchase of the land.
- How much the Trust would agree pay for the bricks and mortar when the prospective member came to move house (a price that would be adjusted for inflation, and for renovations).
- How much the member of the Trust would be expected to pay in land rent.

There is a case for land rents to be regularly updated, to ensure that they stay in line with market values. However, limits to this variation could be built in to ensure both security of tenure for the homeowner and solvency for the Trust. For example, households paying the basic rate of income tax could have their land rent increases capped at the rate of median wage growth.

When moving house, members would sell their bricks and mortar back to the Trust for the rebuild cost. The Trust would then readvertise the bricks and mortar for sale, while retaining the title to the land.

Although the Trust would be non-profit, it would aim to accrue a surplus that would be pooled and used to fund a

Rainy Days and Retirement Discount for members. This would help to improve the attractiveness of the scheme, compared to both renting and the mainstream model of mortgaged home ownership, since it would ensure greater protection for those out of work.

### Governance and finance

The initial capitalisation of the Trust would ideally be financed by government. Reform of property taxation, and the abolition of harmful policies such as Help to Buy, would help to make this possible. Options for the ongoing financing of land acquisitions include borrowing from regional development banks, and bond issue. If the institution benefits from government grants or government-guaranteed borrowing, it is nevertheless important that it remains independent from the state. The Trust would require an executive that is answerable to the members, and a statutory asset lock to ensure that it is more insulated from the whims of future governments.

### Negative equity and debt cancellation

If a government were to come to power in the aftermath of a house price shock, the Trust – with sufficient public backing – could also be a vehicle for helping households that wanted to move house or needed to remortgage, but that were prevented from doing so because they had been pushed into negative equity. Households in negative equity could sell the land from underneath their homes to the Trust at a price that was closer to the pre-crash value, enabling them to pay down their mortgage debt.

In summary, the Trust would offer tangible benefits for:

- **Aspiring homeowners.** The Trust would enable individuals, families and cooperatives with relatively small deposits to enjoy a form of homeownership, and, with that, a degree of security and autonomy over their living space that cannot be provided, even in a reformed private rented sector.

- **Existing homeowners.** The Trust can help to ensure house price stability, by giving the government a lever for supporting demand in the housing market, even while would-be real estate speculators are encouraged to find more productive ways to use their wealth.
- **Private renters.** Through these means, the Trust makes it more politically feasible to bring in rent caps and strengthen rights in the private rented sector, and to clamp down on speculative behaviour that can lead to rapid and ruthless gentrification.

## POLICY IDEA 3

# How do we make occupational pension funds fit for purpose?

*Bruno Bonizzi and Jennifer Churchill*

### What's the issue?

British workers have traditionally relied on occupational pension funds in addition to the state pension to provide their retirement income. These workplace funds are becoming less able to provide income security for all, let alone promote economic growth and financial stability. Reforming the pension system requires an increase in the state pension as well as addressing a number of problems in occupational pensions.

> How could the occupational pension system be reformed so that individual income retirement security can be achieved, alongside promoting economic growth?

### Analysis

In the UK, occupational pension funds have played an important part in the overall provision of retirement income, for higher earners in particular. In many other European countries, recent reforms have been guided by the aspiration of reducing the cost of Pay As You Go state pension benefits, which are financed by current taxation and social insurance contributions. However, in the UK, where state pension benefits are already comparatively low, the focus has been on expanding the coverage of occupational funds, which are pre-funded through contributions accumulated over their working lives, paid for by workers and their employers. This was achieved by the last Labour government for most workers through the introduction of automatic enrolment of workers to an occupational scheme to which, unless they opt out, they contribute a set percentage of their earnings and to which their employers must then also make a minimum contribution. At the same time, the government also set up NEST, a government-administered pension fund for employees of smaller companies who do not have access to a workplace scheme.

There are several so-called 'technical problems' with the new system. Not all workers will accrue benefits. They might work multiple jobs, all below the threshold for employer contributions, or work in precarious employment that does not provide the stability required for pension saving. Current pension schemes are *de facto* individual savings accounts, with tax benefits and employers' contributions, but it is nonetheless difficult to pull separate pots together when moving jobs.

This approach also may not be in the interest of many workers, particularly the low-paid, because it locks money into a pension, unlike savings held in a deposit account, or ISA, to which access is retained at any age in the case of unanticipated financial need. Where wages are low, saving in a pension may be an unaffordable luxury, and workers may opt out even if eligible. For this reason, retaining and increasing the state pension is essential. Entitlement to this should not be on a contributory basis, in order to avoid state pensions reproducing labour market inequalities (for example, by gender).

Moreover, changes to the nature of occupational pension schemes are creating confusion and are progressively shifting financial risk from employers to workers. Defined benefit schemes, in which a guaranteed income based on earnings is paid on retirement, are rapidly closing to new entrants. Most workers now contribute to individual defined contribution funds, where individual benefits on retirement depend on the vagaries of financial markets.

Retirement during financial turbulence or unfavourable financial conditions (for example, a fall in asset prices) can have a significantly negative impact on retirement income. At present there is no protection against this possibility. Pension funds themselves are being pushed towards holding dubious assets in search of yields at a time of low corporate and government investment and low interest rates. There are concerns that pension funds, rather than providing long-term 'patient capital', are fuelling the demand for potentially unstable asset classes. This may be one factor behind the re-emergence of the risky shadow banking sector, as well as being one of the largest sources of financing for hedge funds and private equity funds.

Occupational pensions need to change if they are to provide income security for all working people as they retire and be positive and stabilising factors in financial markets and the economy.

## What can we do?

The following principles should guide the reform of occupational pension schemes:

- **Income security and equity.** Schemes should provide a basic guaranteed income at retirement. This should be complemented with measures to reduce income inequalities by setting guaranteed floors and ceilings in pension payments and/or using public funds to enhance the contributions of poorer workers. Actual benefit payments should exceed the minimum pension, should returns be sufficiently high to pay for this.
- **Sharing the burden.** The risks of retirement provision should not fall entirely on individual workers, as in current individual retirement accounts, or on individual employers, as in traditional final salary schemes. Worker contribution rates and benefits (within the set maximum and minimum

pensions) should be decided on a collective basis, in order to fairly represent the interest of different generations of workers and the long-term financial security of the scheme. Schemes must be large enough so that the risks and costs of retirement can be more effectively shared across workers of all ages and employers.

- **Transparency.** Schemes should be simple and transparent about their workings and cost. They should have a simple contributory structure, and a straightforward calculation of benefits as an annuity with guaranteed rates. This should also make transferring pensions across employers much easier, which is important given the current structure of the labour market.

- **Cost efficiency.** The simple structure of these funds should also work to reduce the costs of their maintenance. These funds should be large enough to realise economies of scale, for example, by having an internal management team, rather than having to rely on costly external managers.

- **Long–term investment strategies.** Pension funds should be oriented towards long-term returns. Given their large size and stable maturity, liquidity to pay current pensioners can be more easily obtained through steady cash inflows from contributions, reducing the need for short-term investment strategies. Pension funds would therefore be 'patient' investors, financing projects the economy needs as well as being stabilising actors in financial markets.

- **Regulation and management.** Regulation should ensure proper management of pension funds, which may include quantitative guidelines on asset allocation. Accounting rules should avoid excessive reliance on accounting procedures that encourage a short-term investment horizon, such as 'mark-to-market' asset and liabilities valuation.

- **Professional management with wide stakeholder representation.** In line with their trust-based structure in the UK, pension funds should ensure effective representation in the decision-making of all stakeholders, especially workers, employers and the state. This is particularly crucial for decisions regarding the size of the benefits above the minimum pension level. Within the mandates given by trustees, the long-term investment horizon and regulatory constraints, actual asset management should be entrusted to (internal) professional managers.

There are several concrete proposals that could be used to develop an occupational pension system in line with these principles. One option is to base it on the so-called 'collective defined contribution' (CDC) pension plans, endorsed by the Trades Union Congress (TUC) and given some support by the parliamentary Work and Pensions Committee, but include minimum (and possibly maximum) pension guarantees. Another proposal is the establishment of local or national government-based Guaranteed Retirement Accounts (GRAs), perhaps by reforming the existing state-sponsored pension scheme NEST.

# POLICY IDEA 4

# How can we stop the social security system aggravating mental distress?

## John Grahl

### What's the issue?

Mentally distressed claimants are being offered simplistic and ineffective remedies and are being pressurised by the social security system to seek employment of any kind, including in poor-quality jobs that can aggravate their mental health conditions.

> How should a progressive government respond to the plight of mentally distressed social security claimants?

### Analysis

Over the last two decades mental health problems have become a key issue in social security policy. This is because, first, unemployment has fallen and benefits for the healthy unemployed are now only a small fraction of social security expenditure. Instead, long-term illness and incapacity makes up a much larger proportion of both caseloads and expenditure. Second, long-term illness itself now predominantly takes the form of mental distress, with anxiety and depression more frequent than physiological problems, such as back pain, which used to account for most sickness-related benefit claims.

In the UK, and in many other advanced economies, social security claims related to illness increased rapidly in the wake of the deindustrialisation of the 1980s. Without questioning the good faith of the claimants, who were certainly unwell, these increases can be interpreted as a form of disguised unemployment in that they would not have risen so rapidly if demand for industrial workers had remained buoyant. The geography of sickness benefits confirms this interpretation: for example, Merthyr Tydfil, devastated by the decline in Welsh heavy industry, was a notorious sickness benefit black spot.

In the 1980s, policy-makers tended to accept the increased sickness benefit bill as the lesser of two evils, preferable to much higher levels of recognised unemployment and providing some compensation to the most vulnerable victims of structural change. However, as high numbers of sickness claims persisted and began to affect more recent generations, governments started to search for ways to limit the cost. Labour market 'inactivity', neither having nor seeking employment (through sickness or for other reasons), was to be discouraged. One sign of this switch was a reformulation of labour market objectives: an increase in employment was now seen as a better target than a reduction in unemployment, because the latter took no account of high rates of inactivity. In the drive to maximise employment, benefit conditions became less supportive of full-time mothers and housewives. From the 1990s on, lone mothers of children at successively younger and younger ages were expected to seek employment, as were all women whose partners claimed benefits. Through the same period, governments also started to make less use of early retirement as a palliative for long-term unemployment.

These changes should not disguise the continuity in both labour market conditions and the nature of incapacity. There has been an alarming rise in mental health problems across Western countries, but the prevalent musculoskeletal disorders may have functioned similarly in the past: in an economy where most jobs were manual they could act as a sickness-induced disqualification from employment in general; in today's service-dominated economy, psychological malfunctions can, in a similar way, indicate an inability to meet the typical constraints of existing labour market conditions.

Thus, the changing forms of sickness in no way undermine the notion of 'disguised unemployment' or, in less tendentious terms, adverse labour market conditions, as a principal source of inactivity. Recent British policy, however, completely inverts this widely accepted causal relationship: current policy is based on the view that the labour market is not the cause of, but rather the remedy for, sickness-related inactivity. This view has led to the imposition of policies towards claimants that needlessly aggravate their distress, while leaving untouched the labour market structures and practices that actually disqualify so many people from employment.

Two main developments have led to the policy impasse: the degeneration of the Universal Credit (UC) 'welfare reform' and the drive within the NHS to address mental health problems through 'Improved Access to Psychiatric Therapies' (IAPT).

The original objective of introducing UC was to simplify the benefit system, by bringing together six of the most important benefits under a single means test, so as to reduce the combined rate at which benefits were withdrawn as claimants re-entered employment or took on more hours of paid work. This should strengthen employment incentives by increasing the gains from taking or increasing employment. On these grounds, UC was widely welcomed by both researchers and organisations concerned with poverty, such as the Joseph Rowntree Foundation and the Child Poverty Action Group (CPAG).

Gradually the welcome gave way to critical concern. After the 2015 General Election the Conservative government confirmed its intention to reduce expenditure on working-age benefits by £12 billion, more than 10 per cent, that is, to claw back some £12 billion per annum from the three largest claimant groups – the unemployed, the chronic sick and the low-paid. It is an indication of social attitudes towards so-called 'welfare' claimants, many of whom are actually in employment, that the Labour opposition did not at that time condemn these cuts and abstained when they were debated in Parliament, although some, including many now in leadership positions in Labour, did vote against them.

These cuts reduced the positive incentives to seek and retain employment. Instead, an increasingly harsh and oppressive treatment of claimants has been substituted to force them into taking employment. The conditions for benefit payments were tightened continually, while breaches of these conditions have been increasingly met with frequent and severe sanctions. Claimants with health problems have been subjected to repeated assessments of their capacity to work – often crudely administered by unqualified staff in the service of revenue-hungry corporations. The assessment process was clearly intended to redesignate as many sickness-related claimants as possible as actually or potentially fit for work.

Unemployed claimants, and those sickness claimants assessed as actually or potentially fit for work, must sign contracts committing them to often futile hours of job search and to participation in often badly designed 'work experience' and training schemes. Provision of these schemes was outsourced to corporations more concerned with profit than providing effective services or accurately reporting on their own performance. The explosion in the numbers resorting to food banks and the destitution caused by arbitrary benefit reductions following from the 'bedroom tax' (the so-called 'spare room subsidy' removal), which disproportionately fell on those with disabilities, both stand as tragic emblems of the increased pressures on claimants.

Meanwhile, wage rates and job security in the labour markets towards which claimants are being impelled have continued to deteriorate. Rather than be sanctioned, claimants are having to accept worse pay and conditions. The continuing roll-out of UC in place of previous benefits means that new and renewed claims will attract substantially lower levels of benefit.

As recognised unemployment continues to fall, the epidemic of mental distress has become ever more central to the drive to reduce spending. Employment and Support Allowance (ESA) and the corresponding sickness-related benefits under UC have become a key item of expenditure, while mental health problems increasingly predominate in these claims, calling into question the cost-effectiveness of the punitive treatment of claimants emerging from the UC reforms. If claimants are suffering from anxiety and/or depression, it is hard to see how suspending their benefits can improve their situation, and growing awareness of the severe consequences of sanctions – including suicides – may well have been a factor behind the unannounced but rapid reduction in the use of sanctions after they reached their peak in 2014.

In this conjuncture, IAPT seemed to offer a silver bullet. Its logic is that mental health problems could be easily overcome because:

- They were individual and not socioeconomic in origin (after all, there are lots of people who do cope).
- Thus, the undeniable correlation between mental distress and socioeconomic disadvantage should be interpreted as showing that mental health problems lead to disadvantage and not the other way around (the welfare reform agenda does not require structural change in the sphere of employment).
- Most psychological problems can be easily dealt with by brief 'talking therapies'.
- Such 'behavioural therapy' is aimed not at improving the socioeconomic situation of the sufferer but simply at altering their patterns of thought so that they cease to dwell on alarming or depressing features of their experience and become – such is the hope – more likely to seek or retain employment.
- No great level of skill or knowledge is required to administer such therapy. It can therefore be provided cheaply.
- This will be cost-effective in promoting employment and reducing benefit claims, since employment promotes psychological wellbeing and mental health.

To a considerable extent, this completely unrealistic approach has displaced serious policy-making about both mental health and the social security system.

## What can we do?

- There is mounting evidence that **current policies are aggravating the material and mental problems of many of the most vulnerable social security claimants.**
- **A complete refocus of policy on the wellbeing of the long-term sick and disabled** is needed in the context of strategies that address the socioeconomic determinants of poor mental health.

# POLICY IDEA 5

# Reconstructing social security

*Simon Deakin*

## What's the issue?

The UK's social security system is both dysfunctional and unjust, not to mention coercive and harsh, in its mode of operation.

> How can we reform the social security system to make it both more efficient and fairer?

## Analysis

All countries beyond a certain level of development have social security systems whose principal task is to manage risks of interruption to income from employment. These can arise from contingencies such as unemployment, sickness and invalidity; life cycle effects, including old age; and family responsibilities. It is no accident that Britain, the first country to industrialise, should have developed, through its 'Poor Law', one of the earliest national social security systems. It's no accident either that, in today's China, the largest ever transition to a market economy is being accompanied by large-scale planning around the issue of social security.

The British Poor Law was often coercive and stigmatising, and many of the features of what became the welfare state began through workers and communities pooling their own resources to manage risks. One policy option for restoring fairness and dignity to unemployment compensation systems would be to devolve this power back to trade unions and bodies similar to the mutual societies of the 19th century. There is, however, a limit to what can be achieved in social security without state intervention. Private insurance markets are not good at protecting high-risk, that is, low-income, groups.

Social insurance schemes around the world continue to operate on the principle of the pooling of contributions, and hence of risks, within the working population, and, by extension, across generations. Just how egalitarian such schemes are depends on matters such as the level of financing, the division of the burden between workers, employers and the state, the strength of the link between contributions and payments, and the conditionality attached to benefits. Also, social insurance schemes can be more or less gender-egalitarian, depending on such factors as how far they assign contribution credits for periods when employment is interrupted by childrearing or other family responsibilities, and whether they are individual- or household-based.

When we compare the UK's current system of social security to how it operated in the relatively recent past (the late 1980s was the turning point), and to systems operating elsewhere, certain features stand out. First, the contributory principle is very weak in the UK. Wage earners in the UK pay National Insurance contributions that are high by international standards in return for benefits that are relatively low as a proportion of income from employment.

Second, and relatedly, contributory benefits fail to provide any real income security. As a result, a major role remains for benefits paid according to need ('means-tested' benefits). Because means testing is complex and can be stigmatising, take-up rates are lower, and transaction costs higher, than would be the case if the contributory system worked effectively. Household means testing also replaces dependency on the state by dependency on a partner, tending to reinforce traditional gender inequalities.

Third, the UK devotes more resources than most other countries do (the US aside) to benefits to support those in employment. The tax credit system, introduced by Conservative governments in the 1980s and significantly expanded by New Labour, provides a supplement to many household incomes. This is a problem because it shifts the cost of providing a living wage from employers to the state.

There are many problems with means testing. It unavoidably means taxing poor households at high marginal rates, as households with rising incomes experience the withdrawal of benefits while, at the same time, their members become liable to pay income tax on their earnings. This both deters low-income earners from seeking out higher-paid work and is unfair, in the sense of inverting the principle, still widely accepted in most of the world, that tax rates should rise progressively with income.

The effect is exacerbated by tax credits that were designed, through supplementing them, to allow wages to be reduced over time, lowering firms' costs. But tax credits send the wrong signal to employers, removing pressure to train workers and deterring capital investment that might increase productivity. While the full story of tax credits has yet to be told, and analysis of their effects continues, they would seem to combine the worst of all worlds, which may account for their lack of take-up outside the UK and US.

Universal Credit (UC), currently being introduced in stages, will not help. On the contrary, it will exaggerate and amplify all the negative features of the regime it is gradually replacing. UC has been designed to make employment more 'attractive' by ensuring that benefit recipients are never better off than those in employment. This logic, for example, is behind the rule delaying the allocation of UC payments to new claimants: because salaries are paid in arrears, to pay UC 'on demand' would, it is argued, treat claimants as a 'privileged' group.

The danger here is that, as conditions attaching to the receipt of state support become more unattractive, the terms and conditions offered by employers to low-wage workers are dragged down in their turn. It was precisely to avoid this kind of downward spiral that social insurance began to replace the Poor Law at the start of the 20th century.

UC is going to cause other severe problems as it is rolled out. At present, sanctions are applied to those receiving benefits, for example, if they unreasonably refuse an offer of work, fail to comply with job search instructions or leave employment without just cause. Recently, benefit sanctions have been running at the rate of over a million cases in some years. Since sanctioning can involve a claimant going without income for several weeks, it is a highly coercive (or, as its designers might say, effective) remedy for perceived failures of labour market 'discipline'. Under UC, sanctioning will be extended for the first time to those who have jobs, as well as the unemployed. For example, credits will be lost if claimants earning below a threshold, based on full-time employment at the National Minimum Wage, do not seek out additional employment. In practice this will mean more bureaucratic micro-management of work–life decisions of low-income households, additional pressure on terms and conditions of employment for already vulnerable groups, and, most likely, a further proliferation of casualised forms of employment including zero-hours contracts.

Thus, the UK's harsh and dysfunctional social security system is also one of the main causes of low-paid, precarious and casual work. Policy-makers defend the system on the grounds that it has contributed to the UK's much-vaunted labour market flexibility. That defence is correct as long as it is remembered that 'flexible' is really just another way of saying 'precarious', and that precarious employment, while profitable for some employers, is costly for workers, families and the state.

## What can we do?

- There are two routes to changing this unfair but also inefficient system. One, increasingly advocated by some researchers and popular in the media, is the idea of a **Universal Basic Income** (UBI). There is a case for some universal benefits; child benefit was until recently paid for all children irrespective of parental income and had near-universal take-up. Universalism avoids the imposition of high marginal tax rates on poorer recipients, while necessitating their imposition on the better-off (as this is the most effective way to finance it).

- **Merging all existing benefits into a 'general' UBI** would be a very different step. As 'How could Universal Basic Income (UBI) improve social security?' (Policy idea 6, this part of the book) shows, income tax would have to rise very steeply to support a UBI that was sufficient to provide a level adequate for all households to live on. Most worryingly, in the absence of universal collective bargaining or a minimum wage set at an unprecedentedly high level, a UBI would send the wrong signal to employers, who would use it to justify cutting wages. A general UBI, replacing employment-based social security, is just not plausible in an economy characterised by wage labour, which, for the foreseeable future, is the reality that policy-makers must confront.

- The alternative to a general UBI is a **revived social insurance system**. This would entail restoring the link between contributions and earnings, phasing out means testing, and withdrawing the subsidy effect of tax credits and UC. This could work if, at the same time, there was a restoration of effective wage regulation through sector-level collective bargaining, and a return to a demand-led macroeconomic policy that had stable employment as its goal. Far from being unattainable or alien to conditions in the UK, this mix of policies was precisely what lay behind the Beveridge Report of 1942 and the Full Employment White Paper of 1944. The gendered assumptions of the Beveridge Report would not survive scrutiny today. But, as noted above, social insurance schemes can be designed to be gender-neutral, or, going further, to offset the effects of discrimination in employment. Since social insurance and full employment policy together delivered three decades of economic growth alongside steady redistribution of incomes and wealth, perhaps it is time to take a fresh look at them.

# How could Universal Basic Income (UBI) improve social security?

*Stewart Lansley and Howard Reed*

## What's the issue?

A Universal Basic Income (UBI), a tax-free weekly income paid to every individual as of right, would tackle one of the key weaknesses of the social security system – its failure to build a guaranteed income floor. A UBI would, for the first time, provide such a floor, while reducing poverty, inequality and the number of people on means-tested benefits.

> Would a basic income programme that reduced poverty, inequality and the use of means-tested benefits be feasible and affordable?

## Analysis

Critics argue that an affordable scheme would be inadequate, and an adequate scheme would be unaffordable. To assess this, we modelled two different approaches:

- A full scheme with generous payments to replace most, although not all, benefits. Simulations show that such a scheme would either be too expensive or create too many low-income losers, and would not be feasible in the current circumstances.
- A partial scheme to provide a universal and unconditional income at a moderate starting level, leaving much of the existing system intact. This would be feasible. Payments could be set at £51 for pensioners, £71 for adults over 25, £61 for those under 25, and £59 for children. The basic income for children would replace child benefit, but most other benefits – such as those for people with disabilities – would remain. UBI payments would be considered as income when calculating means-tested benefits.

The second, partial scheme, requires three key changes to the existing tax/benefit system to reduce its costs:

- The personal tax allowance (of no benefit to those with earnings below the tax threshold) would be replaced by the flat-rate UBI payment to all.
- Marginal income tax rates would be increased, with the basic and higher rates rising from their current 20 per cent and 40 per cent to 25 per cent and 45 per cent, respectively.
- National Insurance lower and upper earnings limits would be abolished and the rate of employee National Insurance contributions increased to 12 per cent throughout the earnings scale.

## What can we do?

Such a partial scheme would offer real and substantial gains:

- **a sharp increase in income among the poorest**;
- **a 45 per cent cut in child poverty**;
- **a modest reduction in inequality**; and
- **a strengthening of the universal element of the social support system**, leading to a 20 per cent fall in the number of households claiming means-tested benefits.

These changes produce a more progressive and integrated tax–benefit system, with reductions in poverty and inequality, a strengthening of universalism and more means testing shifted to the tax system.

The partial scheme has a net annual cost of £8 billion, just under 0.5 per cent of GDP. This is calculated by netting off the increased income from income tax and National Insurance contributions (£160.6 billion), and reduced spending on other benefits and tax credits (£40.7 billion) from the gross cost of paying UBI to all individuals in the UK (£209.5 billion).

Compared to overall public spending, £8 billion is a modest sum to pay for the substantial reduction in poverty and inequality. By one widely used measure (proportion of children in households falling below 60 per cent of median net household income, before housing costs) child poverty would be reduced to a level last seen in the 1970s.

The results are based on a static analysis, assuming no behavioural effects in response to the introduction of UBI and the tax changes. In practice, there would be dynamic and progressive behavioural effects, as a UBI would provide, for the first time, financial support for the mass of currently unpaid work and, crucially, give individuals greater freedom of choice between work, leisure, education and caring. However, while such a scheme would retain some of the complexity of the existing system, it would create an unconditional income floor, boost the incomes of the poorest and deliver a number of key improvements over the existing social security system.

## POLICY IDEA 7

# Would Universal Basic Income (UBI) address the causes of inequality, ill-being and injustice?

*Ian Gough*

### What's the issue?

This policy idea evaluates Universal Basic Income (UBI) as a solution to the problems of the modern welfare state and its social protection system.

> Could a feasible Universal Basic Income (UBI) payment successfully replace a substantial part of the welfare system?

### Analysis

The British welfare state is an evolving institutional complex comprising state programmes in cash and in kind, such as public services, a tax system, numerous forms of intervention in the labour market and public regulation of enterprises, households and other actors. Public expenditure on the welfare state amounts to about £700 billion, 26 per cent of GDP. Of this £700 billion, about one-half comprises cash transfers to households. The remaining half comprises direct government spending on health and education, personal social services, housing etc, including a rapidly growing proportion on contracted-out services and quasi-markets.

The welfare state has been subject to four decades of cuts, privatisation and restructuring with overtly regressive goals. Despite these obstacles and attacks, the welfare system persists and continues to pursue progressive goals, citizenship needs and rights rather than private interests, as illustrated in Table 1.

Reform is no simple task. In the last few years there has been a groundswell of support in the labour movement and the green movement for a single radical reform, a Universal Basic Income (UBI) or Citizen's Income, an unconditional payment made to every individual as a right of citizenship. It could be paid to everyone on a monthly basis and aim to provide 'a basic amount on which every citizen can survive, excluding housing and any extra costs for disability living'.

See 'Investing in social infrastructure' (Part Two, Policy idea 6), for further discussion of what constitutes 'investment' and 'infrastructure'.

*Arguments for UBI*

The most important claims in favour of UBI are as follows. First, UBI would provide more freedom of choice, a better work–life balance, enhancement of gender equality and expand choices between paid and unpaid work. Second, it would provide a solution to the mass unemployment that many argue will result from automation. Third, it would reduce the employment insecurity of young people. Fourth, a universal minimum would overcome the problem of losing benefits when taking on or increasing employment. Fifth, it would be 'minimally presumptuous', in that a UBI entails no official enquiries into a person's activities or household arrangements, in contrast to assistance benefits in many welfare systems.

**Table 1:** The progressive goals and activities of social policy

|  | Welfare goals | Typical existing social programmes |
|---|---|---|
| Redistribution | Guarantee a minimum income<br>Improve income security<br>Reduce inequality | Cash transfers to individuals and households, including social insurance, income-related and tax benefit programmes<br>Taxation and 'fiscal welfare', a major redistributive instrument |
| Social consumption | Collective provision for basic needs<br>Regulate and reduce harmful consumption | Social services in kind: free or subsidised access to health services, social care, housing<br>Regulation and prevention: modifying social behaviour and patterns of consumption |
| Social investment | Develop human and social capabilities<br>Provide decent paid employment and opportunities for all forms of social participation | Education, training, equal opportunities, and part of health and social care provision*<br>Employment policies, ranging from 'full employment' policy, labour market regulation and wages policies, to 'activation' and working time reduction programmes<br>Social engagement programmes |

*See 'Investing in social infrastructure' (Policy idea 6, Part Two of this book) for further discussion of what constitutes 'investment' and 'infrastructure'.

*Arguments against UBI*

At first sight UBI appears to embody Marx and Engels' goal of communism: 'From each according to his abilities, to each according to his needs'. Indeed, it was once hailed as 'the capitalist road to communism'. However, UBI involves the fallacy of substituting a single policy instrument for a broad policy goal.

In as far as UBI seeks to be a reform of the social security tax and transfer system, it does not address the social consumption and social investment functions of the welfare state. These functions make a vital contribution to need satisfaction and wellbeing, social solidarity, equity and social sustainability. Right-wing supporters favour UBI as a route to dismantling welfare states, by giving everyone an income to buy their own marketised services and thus allowing 'customers choice'. A progressive agenda must search out policies to achieve several goals beyond consumer choice, including equity and sustainability.

Collectively provided public services, such as education and health, available to all according to need, tend to be inclusive and egalitarian. They constitute a very substantial social income that is highly redistributive. On average across OECD (Organisation for Economic Co-operation and Development) countries, the value of public services makes up 76 per cent of the final income of the poorest groups (after taxes and benefits and including the value of such 'benefits in kind') and just 14 per cent for the richest. This social contribution to income reduces income inequality by 20 per cent (see Seery, 2014). In today's political climate, a basic income could threaten resources currently devoted to public services and intensify the effects that 'austerity' policies have had on the post-war welfare settlement.

Any UBI scheme will be either inadequate or unaffordable – as is recognised by its advocates. The Citizen's Income Trust ruled out the possibility of a Full Citizen's Income for everyone as far too expensive. This is because of the arithmetic: if a 20 per cent tax rate is needed to pay for all other government spending, then a basic income set at 50 per cent of average income would require a total tax share of 70 per cent.

Thus, *all* extant proposals envisage a Partial Basic Income with benefits well below the poverty line and the current minimum wage. One such is outlined in 'How could Universal Basic Income (UBI) improve social security?' (Policy idea 6, this part of the book), which is admirably honest in demonstrating how small its benefits are given the uplift in taxation required to fund it. Child poverty would be cut substantially, although this could be more efficiently achieved by raising child benefit. Pensioner and working-age adult poverty would diminish by derisory amounts, despite working-age poverty being a basic target of UBI. Moreover, many of the eligibility criteria and entitlement terms that UBI seeks to do away with would need to be retained, with the numbers reliant on means testing predicted to fall by only one-fifth. Four-fifths would continue to face the indignities of claiming social benefits, and therefore not experiencing the rights-based welfare, non-presumptuousness and simplicity that UBI is supposed to deliver.

Notwithstanding these problems, UBI is increasingly advocated on the left as a mobilising slogan to bring about radical change. This has not so far proved to be the case anywhere in the world, but is it possible that a more globalised and insecure world could bring this about? This seems doubtful.

UBI is an individualistic, monetary intervention that does not in itself encourage social solidarity or address the underlying causes of poverty, unemployment and inequality. The problem of changing labour relations and reducing precarious employment are not directly addressed by a basic income. According to Cruddas and Kibasi (2016), UBI 'institutionalises the gap between the disproportionate and increasing rewards for the few and stagnant wages and poor prospects for the many.... Issues of class, economic ownership and the productive capacity of the economy are collapsed into lazy utopian remedies.'

## What can we do?

- **UBI requires a top-down abolition of numerous social support programmes and their replacement with a single payment.** Policy experience indicates that there is rarely a simple relationship between instruments and outcomes, and that 'one-size-fits-all' policies rarely succeed.
- A more effective policy approach would be **to address directly the underlying causes of inequalities, ill-being and injustice.** Reducing these sources of inequality requires expanding a range of interventions of the social democratic welfare state. These interventions include labour market reform, as well as investing in public services and other forms of social consumption.

# Interlude: What is 'social' infrastructure – and why does it matter so much?

Sue Konzelmann and Marc Fovargue-Davies

We all know what infrastructure is; after all, we drive on roads and go to schools and hospitals pretty much every day. But what exactly is 'social' infrastructure?

One way to look at it is as the 'software' – like the transport, education, health and social care systems – that make us all able to live together. Social infrastructure is the collective contribution to our wellbeing, mostly provided by and for people but funded by the state, although exactly how varies from situation to situation. What it's good at is making life that bit easier and getting the best out of people. That means you'll also really notice the hole it leaves when it's not there – and that's what happens when funding for it is cut.

By 2015, inequality in the UK had reached the point where the 100 richest people had as much wealth as 18 per cent of the entire population. Perhaps unsurprisingly, this also meant that some 14 million people – 4.5 million of them children – were now living below the poverty line. And public spending on their schools, their childcare and their housing had fallen too. That will seriously impact their life chances, making it very difficult for them to escape poverty for the rest of their lives. This makes a pretty strong case for investing collectively in things that will help them – and as a result, the economy – out.

However, instead of being invested in to help those struggling with poverty at critical stages, our social infrastructure has been rapidly hollowed out. Since the coalition government took office in 2010, public services, council funding, benefit entitlements, school budgets and student maintenance grants have all been cut.

Aside from the more obvious results – such as schools being able to provide far less help for children who fall behind – what does this poverty actually look like? In an interview with *The Guardian* in April 2018, the headteacher of a primary school in Nottingham made it clear that it was about rather more than not having 'on-trend' trainers:

> We have a food bank, so we give out food parcels, particularly on Fridays, we buy clothing, we do a lot of buying, particularly coats in winter and shoes. We've had children who haven't come to school because they didn't have shoes. We've gone and bought shoes, taken them to their house and brought the child into school. (Adams, 2018)

Another headteacher, quoted in the same article, was shocked by the contrast in the appearance of her own pupils and those from schools with better-off children:

> My children, who have gone from me up to the local secondary school, have grey skin, poor teeth, poor hair, poor nails. They are smaller, they are thinner. At sporting events, you see your children in the year group compared to other children in an affluent area and you think: our kids are really small. You don't notice it because you're with them all the time, but when you see them with children of the same age who are from an affluent area, they just look tiny. (Adams, 2018)

The last time something like this was seen in the UK was over a century ago – when it was obvious that a high proportion of British men were unfit to serve in the Boer War. The conditions producing those undersized, would-be soldiers were those of the 19th century – before any form of state-run welfare was in place in Britain. The result of failing to invest in social infrastructure is therefore clear – and certainly shouldn't come as a surprise.

Not only does it produce more people with inadequate resources to improve their lot; it gives them a less-than-healthy start in life too. Nor is that the end of the bad news, since social infrastructure problems aren't restricted to children and education, but negatively influence health, social care and communities as well. Cutting these kinds of services can only be false economy – a phrase that could probably also sum up the UK's economic strategy since 1980.

# Part Five:
# How to provide for social needs

## Introduction

*Susan Himmelweit*

People's standard of living depends not only on their incomes, but also on the level and standard of public services they have access to. Indeed, for the poorest households and those that use public services the most, benefits and public services – 'benefits in kind' – contribute a larger proportion of their standard of living than their own earnings. Austerity policies have therefore had a particularly catastrophic impact on the living standards of those who are most dependent on public services, such as those with a disability, older people and children.

But attacks on public services were happening long before the financial crash and subsequent austerity policies. Many previously publicly provided services had been contracted out to private sector providers, even when still publicly funded. The ostensible reason for such marketisation varied for different types of services, but invariably part of the justification rested on a claim that private provision was more efficient, and so through lower costs would save 'taxpayers' money'. It was not so frequently recognised that those lower costs arose, at least in part, from private providers being able to employ a more casualised, less unionised and often less skilled workforce than the public sector.

Citizens have also been persuaded to see themselves as consumers, benefiting from being able to exercise choice, fuelling competition between providers in delivering value for money. Some previously public services have been almost entirely replaced by individual budgets. These enable, and in some cases force, eligible recipients, such as those with disabilities, to exercise choice as to how to spend the budget they are given. However, with budgets not high enough to allow much freedom, such choice is more illusory than real. One outcome has been a decline in collective provision and increased loneliness as individual budgets are spent on individualised services.

Further, it has proved easy to allow the real value of individual budgets to be eroded (much easier, perhaps, than to do so to the pay of unionised public sector workers). As a result, deteriorating workers' conditions, through, for example, the increasing use of zero-hours contracts, have provided gains in efficiency, but have not benefited the recipients of public services. Rather, they have enabled expenditure to be reduced, or not to grow in line with the rising needs of an ageing population.

Particular conditions need to be fulfilled for consumer choice and competition to push up quality of provision. Where quality is hard to assess, or change difficult to make, as in residential care, for example, competition tends, in practice, to be over price alone, and consumers are often stuck with unsuitable provision because choices once made are too costly to change. In many services, competition among private for-profit providers simply results in poor quality, with cost reductions in highly labour-intensive services inevitably being taken out in the pay and conditions of workers.

Almost 40 years of devotion to such free market policies, by both Conservative and New Labour governments, has resulted in their application in almost all public services, regardless of their suitability. This part of the book looks at several areas that are particularly unsuited to such marketisation, and it considers alternative policy ideas on how a revived and recast public sector might better meet individual needs with beneficial effects on the economy and society more widely. It concentrates particularly on the health service, social care and childcare, and on education.

It is important to revive the idea of public services as contributing to the public good, because, after years of inappropriate reforms and under-investment, public services have taken a beating in the public imagination. Instead, we need a view of them as an investment in all our futures, in our social infrastructure, just as much as the policies more recognisably about industrial policy discussed in Part Two. A reassertion of the value of public provision should be not just about nationalising traditional areas of physical infrastructure but about our public services too.

The policy ideas in this part concentrate on how to have 21st-century public services that are once again run for the public good. Leslie Huckfield starts by considering how successive governments have steered non-profit 'social' providers towards profit generation, undermining their focus on social objectives. He suggests a way to manage a transition back to public provision based on genuine non-profit principles.

The next four policy ideas focus on health and social care. Pauline Allen argues that attempts to introduce market-like mechanisms into the NHS have failed to deliver enhanced efficiency, quality or accountability. She proposes an alternative 'hierarchical' public sector that could improve accountability and decision-making, reduce transaction costs and improve fair access. Kate Pickett argues that successive UK governments have failed to tackle the structural social factors that cause increasing health inequalities, and suggests 10 wide-ranging proposals to do so. Jane Lethbridge argues that social care provision is underfunded, undervalued, insufficiently responsive to individual needs and pursuing the wrong goals. She proposes a centrally funded National Care Service driven by the needs of local people. Then Dean Baker suggests how strategic public investment in the pharmaceuticals industry could prevent drug prices from continuing to take an ever-increasing share of the nation's health budget.

The remaining three policy ideas focus on childcare and education. Jerome De Henau argues that investing in high-quality, universal, public sector childcare provision is not only desirable for children, their parents and the childcare profession but, even ignoring its long-term benefits, also generates employment that substantially reduces the net cost of such investment in the short term. Francis Green and David Kynaston then emphasise the importance of tackling public schools to create a socially just education system, and propose a solution to progressively undermine the private/state divide and its divisive consequences. Finally, Liz Marr proposes a number of changes that could go some way towards reversing the decline in adult part-time study and make lifelong learning a reality for all, an issue that will be of increasing importance in the future working lives of us all.

## Policy ideas

1. How can we stop privatisation of public services? *Leslie Huckfield*
2. What has the market done to the English NHS and with what should we replace it? *Pauline Allen*
3. What's the best way to tackle health inequalities? *Kate Pickett*
4. What's the best way of delivering social care? *Jane Lethbridge*
5. How do we make drug prices an easier pill for the NHS to swallow? *Dean Baker*
6. How much would high-quality childcare cost and how would we pay for it? *Jerome De Henau*
7. What should be done about private schools? *Francis Green and David Kynaston*
8. How do we make lifelong learning a reality for all? *Liz Marr*

# POLICY IDEA 1

# How can we stop privatisation of public services?

*Leslie Huckfield*

## What's the issue?

UK outsourcing, or external procurement, is now huge in scale, and channels a significant proportion of national and local public budgets. In 2014/15 the UK spent almost one-third of total government expenditure on external suppliers. Past governments' efforts to steer this spending towards non-profit 'social' providers, such as social enterprises and cooperatives, have not relieved the pressure to monetise and commercialise outsourced services, steering them towards profit generation and undermining their focus on social need.

What policy should a progressive government apply to public sector procurement in order to end overt and covert privatisation of public services?

## Analysis

From 1997, the concept of 'social enterprise' was promoted by New Labour as a welfare reform initiative, because 'the welfare state's capacity to meet modern social problems is limited'. Since then, a raft of New Labour and Conservative funding and policies have facilitated delivery of public services by the 'third sector' organisations with distinct forms of ownership, governance and motivation that operate alongside the public and private sectors. More than £1 billion has now been spent by government and the Big Lottery Fund to subsidise social investment, using private funds, in third sector delivery.

Third sector organisations include social enterprises (accountable to a community or charitable organisation), cooperatives (owned by their employees) and mutuals (owned by their customers as shareholders). Although they claim they are different through seeking to cover their costs while donating or reinvesting any surplus, depending on their structure, some do distribute profits to external investors. Although opposed by many in the cooperative movement, one of the motivations for community interest companies, introduced by New Labour in 2004, was to allow private investment and distribution to investors.

The claim made by this range of 'social organisations', often heightened by their being embedded in communities they serve, is their potential to combine the public sector's social purpose with a focus on efficient service delivery and satisfying customer demand. However, many in central and local government now view them simply as low-cost delivery structures, not least because of their exploitation of the voluntary labour and non-financial motivations of their workforce. For public sector workers, outsourcing to these third sector organisations for local government and NHS delivery now represents just as big a threat as outsourcing to the private sector.

The expanding role of third sector providers in public procurement has been actively promoted by a range of policies and programmes, including work on:

- Article 77 of the EU Procurement Directive, transposed into UK Public Procurement Regulations, which mandates open competition with the private sector after an initial three-year contract reserved for third sector organisations.
- The Social Services and Wellbeing (Wales) Act 2014, which gives local authorities a duty to promote social enterprises and cooperatives.
- Social investment bonds, first launched by Labour in 2010, encourage private investment in 'social organisations'. These pay dividends when output targets, such as deporting London homeless and rough sleepers back to their own countries, are met, making the delivery of public services dominated by the returns sought by investors.
- A wide range of other programmes and proposals, from Big Society Capital and The National Lottery Community Fund, to which the Big Lottery Fund has now changed its name, support for social impact bonds and social investment, funding from the Department of Health for social prescribing, to initiatives from the Co-operative Councils Innovation Network, Co-operatives UK, New Economics Foundation, NESTA and others.

The intention of these outsourcing proposals – initiated by New Labour but expanded by successive Conservative governments – is to reduce public spending by ensuring that the public purse pays no more than the marginal cost of delivery, leaving the delivery organisation to fund set-up, development and other costs, increasingly from private sources. This means that a 'third sector' organisation itself has to raise private funds through loans and equity to deliver public services. The cumulative effect is stimulation of a market in public service delivery, in which 'social enterprises' compete with (and behave as) private enterprises.

Under the Conservative government's interpretation of the EU Procurement Directive above, rushed through before the May 2015 General Election, it is legally possible in some markets, including health, social, cultural, personal, educational and training services, to restrict suppliers to specific 'qualifying organisations' that meet or will meet 'if and when it performs the contract' the following criteria:

- pursuing a public service mission;
- reinvesting profits, or distributing them based on participatory considerations;
- having structures of management based on employee ownership or participatory principles.

The insertion of 'if and when it performs the contract' means that a private for-profit company may bid and then become a 'qualifying organisation' only if it wins the contract. The way this is defined also enables a local authority to spin out its own services from the public sector.

A range of private and third sector structures is emerging within this marketised approach. In 2010, the Cabinet Office defined a new variant – 'public service mutuals' – as 'an organisation which has left the public sector ... but continues to deliver public services' (Mutuals Taskforce, 2012). It is claimed that 'employee control plays a significant role in their operation' (Mutuals Taskforce, 2012). But this does not mean that these mutuals are controlled by former public sector employees. As an example, the Civil Service Pensions Department was effectively privatised in 2012 by turning it into MyCSP, a 'mutual joint venture' in which the private Equiniti Group owned 40 per cent, the government 35 per cent and employees 25 per cent. But the government subsequently sold part of its share, leaving Equiniti with a controlling stake in the organisation that administers the UK civil service pension scheme. More such privatisations will follow.

An earlier Labour government, through the Industrial Common Ownership Act 1976, created at least 2,000 cooperatives, which practised economic democracy within a wider social economy to defend communities and jobs. But these were not promoted to deliver public services. In a major rupture with the wider cooperative movement, the first two New Labour governments of 1997 and 2001 reinstitutionalised third sector organisations to become deliverers of low-cost public services. Under New Labour and the Conservatives, third sector organisations have long been under political and financial pressure to accept a bigger role in service delivery, as well as moral pressure to step in where other public provision falls short of need. This has understandably conditioned third sector organisations and social entrepreneurs to view ongoing outsourcing not only as an opportunity for expansion, but also as a mainstream way of raising funding. Rather than creating nurturing 'public–social partnerships', many now compete against the private sector in a race to the bottom to win service delivery contracts by cutting wages and jobs.

## What can we do?

- The current scale of third sector organisations' involvement, and the type of management approach imposed on them, requires a **carefully managed transition back to public provision based on genuine non-profit principles**. Since this will take time and resources, a progressive government must redesign public procurement models to prevent a commercialisation that solely focuses on cost reduction. There are various precedents that show how this might be done.
- One example of an alternative approach, in health and social care, is the **Better Government for Older People** (BGOP) programme, funded by Labour in 1998 to oversee 28 research projects for the engagement of older people in a variety of services. As a national action research initiative, it was steered jointly by a government department, a university research consortium and four charitable organisations. As an example, the programme in Devon included work on:
  - engaging older people in the Exeter City best value programme and Mid Devon locality GP commissioning group national pilot;
  - employment prospects for the over-50s in a rural area;
  - engaging older people in planning and community profiling initiatives;
  - recruiting older volunteers as peer researchers on users' views of community reablement;
  - the authority's own position as an employer of older people;

– enabling older people to take more control of the services they require.

- The emerging **Fair Care model** brought together people engaged in giving and receiving care, including workers, informal carers and, importantly, people traditionally labelled 'service users'. Fair Care coops sought to develop a 'circle of care' for each. These are one tested alternative to the marketised commissioning and procurement system in which each service user receives person-centred support, through controlling their own care, in a mutual setting, while sharing responsibility for the wellbeing of other members, including workers and unpaid carers.

- Another example being piloted and supported in Scotland is **public social partnerships**, under which public and third sector organisations work together to find new ways of delivery, involving service providers and users.

- Finally, the funds from programmes that currently support private funding for public service delivery could be redirected into **local economic democracy projects**, which could be bid for by groups bringing together service users, statutory providers, trade unions and, where relevant, third sector organisations to provide services currently outsourced to the private sector.

- Above all, a progressive government should consider **returning cooperatives, mutuals, social enterprises and third sector organisations to their original function of providing and creating jobs, community support and self-defence**.

# POLICY IDEA 2

# What has the market done to the English NHS and with what should we replace it?

*Pauline Allen*

### What's the issue?

The introduction of market-like mechanisms into the English NHS since 1990 has failed to generate the benefits of enhanced efficiency, quality and accountability that market competition was supposed to deliver. As well as enabling fair access, an alternative hierarchical institutional structure for healthcare governance could improve accountability, allow efficient decision-making and reduce transaction costs.

> Should we replace the existing NHS 'quasi-market' with a more hierarchical structure?

### Analysis

The logic behind introducing market mechanisms into the NHS relies on the idea of a 'perfect' market, and how such an ideal type of market is meant to work. A market for a good or service is said to be perfect when competition is sufficient to ensure that the amount produced and the price at which it is purchased are 'optimal', in that the demand by well-informed purchasers prepared to pay that price can be satisfied by producers able to make a profit and therefore willing to sell at that price. Competition adjusts the market price until the demand expressed by purchasers is exactly met by the supply provided by the most efficient producers. Large numbers of both informed buyers and rational providers are required for competition to operate in this way.

In perfect markets, not only is efficiency assumed to be achieved: so is accountability. This is because each consumer is assumed to make their own decisions based on adequate information, providers are rational in making production decisions that maximise their profits, and the terms of the agreement between consumer and provider can be enforced by contract law.

However, such theories of perfect markets do not concern themselves with issues relating to fairness in the distribution of goods and services.

In contrast to markets, many public services are organised in hierarchies within which those at the top have most authority, with progressively less authority vested in each level below. Rather than purchasing services from the market, governments collect taxes and use these resources to produce and allocate services. One reason for this arrangement is that balancing the needs of different groups of people is important in the allocation of public services; hierarchies are required to make decisions on behalf of us all that take these different needs into account.

The market form introduced into the NHS was a 'quasi-market' that sought to combine the supposed advantages of competition between suppliers while retaining public funding to safeguard fairness in access to healthcare. A market was introduced by means of a split between the providers of healthcare and its purchasers (known as 'commissioners'), being other parts of the state acting on behalf of patients. Public sector providers have been constituted into relatively autonomous, publicly owned, 'self-governing trusts' that are supposed to compete with each other and are thereby presumed to be enhancing technical efficiency by ensuring 'value for money', that is, delivering the highest feasible level of output for any resources used. Non-state providers have also been encouraged to enter the market. Decisions about the purchase of healthcare are made by commissioners, and the system of annual budget allocations to hospitals was replaced with one based on negotiated contracts between commissioners and providers.

While a quasi-market was seen by some as the best solution for providing efficient and high-quality healthcare, economic and legal theory suggests that serious problems could be encountered in moving to such a system from the pre-existing hierarchical arrangement.

There is unlikely to be a high degree of competition in the provision of healthcare, especially between specialist hospitals and in sparsely populated areas. Moreover, as it is impossible to monitor all aspects of healthcare performance, unless prices are fixed, competition can be expected to reduce quality, as providers find ways of skimping on unobserved aspects of healthcare quality in order to lower their costs. Attempting to avoid this problem, fixed prices were introduced gradually into the NHS quasi-market from 2003/04, in the expectation that competition would be based on quality alone. However, skimping on non-observable aspects of quality may still occur. Further, difficulties may arise in fixing an appropriate price: if the price is too low, providers may be encouraged to skimp on quality to reduce costs and become more 'efficient', and, if the price is too high, there is no incentive for providers to become more efficient.

The inability to monitor all aspects of healthcare affects more than price setting; it also has the potential to undermine the effective use of contracts in healthcare markets, both in increasing efficiency and in achieving accountability. Because the transaction costs of contracting for healthcare are significant, once these are taken into account, the increased efficiency produced by market competition is debatable. In healthcare contracting, the very difficulties that lead to high transactions costs also cause problems in using such contracts to achieve full accountability from providers. Not being able to monitor all aspects of performance, the use of markets as a method for improving accountability is unlikely to be effective.

Thus, there are potential advantages in retaining hierarchy as the institutional structure for healthcare, because, when market incentives cannot be effectively harnessed for the public good, they can be detrimental to efficiency and quality of care. For-profit providers who enter the market have strong incentives to skimp on quality to increase their profits.

## Evidence on the operation of the quasi-market in the English NHS

Since the introduction of a quasi-market into the English NHS, there has not been a high degree of competition between hospitals. Where price competition has taken place, quality of care has deteriorated. On the other hand, there is some (disputed) evidence that quality of care may have improved in the context of competition under fixed prices.

The degree to which organisations providing care are free to make their own decisions matters in markets. Autonomy is assumed to engender more efficient and higher quality care, as those running the organisations know best how to respond effectively to patient need and demand. However, evidence from the more autonomous NHS hospitals – foundation trusts (FTs) – that were introduced by New Labour does not bear this out. Moreover, there is no evidence to suggest that independent providers – whether for-profit or otherwise – are performing better (or, indeed, worse) than NHS-owned organisations.

'Command and control' hierarchical measures have continued to operate concurrently in the English NHS. These mechanisms are necessary because they are central to achieving NHS goals of continuity of care for patients (which requires cooperation between providers), meeting national standards for quality and keeping the whole NHS within nationally set financial limits. In practice, FT autonomy has been severely circumscribed, and the national NHS hierarchy still has a strong influence on FT decision-making.

The Health and Social Care Act 2012 has been seen as a high-water mark of pro-market policies for the NHS. Although the Act contains attempts to increase the power of market mechanisms, mainly through promotion of competition and non-state provider market entry, these efforts have been attenuated by provisions aimed at ensuring that other important goals of the NHS (such as integration and continuity of care) are still taken into account. What is more, since 2014, the NHS has been focusing on improving cooperation between local organisations rather than using market mechanisms to achieve goals of better value for money and improved quality of care.

## What can we do?

- It is not possible to construct a healthcare market conforming to classical economic principles. Nor is it desirable to do so, as markets in healthcare cannot deliver crucial goals such as fairness of access or value for money. In this context, a **hierarchy is preferable**.
- In the English political environment, central government will inevitably be held politically responsible for health services. A hierarchical governance structure provides the **state** the best opportunity to exercise **control over the NHS**, which will, in turn, **improve accountability**.
- Further, a hierarchy allows s**trategic planning and allocatively efficient decisions to take place at the appropriate level** of aggregation.
- Finally, such governance structures are also likely to be efficient in **reducing transactions costs** for complex services.

# POLICY IDEA 3

# What's the best way to tackle health inequalities?

*Kate Pickett*

**What's the issue?**

The UK has the longest and strongest tradition of research on the social determinants of health and health inequalities of any country, more government papers and reports, and more policy. Yet British governments have struggled to reduce inequalities in health.

> What policies would be most effective in reducing health inequalities?

**Analysis**

The Labour governments of 1997–2010 pursued a comprehensive programme to reduce health inequalities, and made progress in doing so. Their 1999 plan, *Reducing Health Inequalities: An Action Report* (Macintyre, 1999), adopted many of the recommendations from the 1998 Independent Inquiry into Inequalities in

Health. Their economic and social policies included a national minimum wage, higher benefits and pensions, the 'Sure Start' programme, health action zones and increased spending on education, housing, health and urban regeneration. In 2001, the government set targets for health inequalities with the goal of narrowing differences in life expectancy across geographic areas and in infant mortality across social classes. From 2002 to 2010, it published a series of reviews and action plans to tackle health inequalities, culminating in the 2010 Marmot Review, *Fair Society, Healthy Lives* (Marmot, 2010).

The most recent research on inequalities in health in England, published by Barr, Higgerson and Whitehead in the *British Medical Journal* in 2017 (Barr, 2017), assessed trends in life expectancy in three periods: before the 2003 Programme for Action, during the implementation of the programme, and subsequently in the coalition/Conservative era. The analysis shows clearly that the programme was associated with a decline in geographical inequalities in life expectancy that reversed a previously increasing trend. Since the programme ended, inequalities have started to increase again.

A growing body of evidence, published in top medical journals, demonstrates the impact of austerity on population health since 2010, including a shocking rise in infant mortality among the poorest social classes, and an alarming increase in the North–South divide in death rates for adults aged 25–44. The evidence indicates that there have been tens of thousands of excess deaths among the elderly, increasing numbers of suicides and the end of a century-long rise in life expectancy.

These research findings on the damage caused by inequality and austerity should be used to call for progressive economic and social policies that support population health and reduce inequalities. Surveys show that the British public are consistently concerned about the NHS, health and social care.

The government, faced with evidence that health inequalities are widening, and health gains being reversed, point to international rankings that place the NHS at the top of health services (although there are other rankings that place it much lower). However, it is not just health services that shape public health, but social conditions too. The NHS requires greater resources, but this should not be separated from the need for economic and social policies that reduce both poverty and inequality, important measures to improve public health and wellbeing. It is immoral that the fifth largest economy in the world is failing to protect the health of not only the most vulnerable citizens and residents, but of all of us.

## What can we do?

Progressive economic and social policies are needed to provide the **tax-based resources for increased investment in health and social care** and, by reducing poverty and inequality, to directly benefit the health of the whole population.

The top policy proposals from a survey of public health experts aim to **reduce poverty and inequality and ensure a better quality of life for everyone**. The consensus is that the structural social determinants of health matter the most; there is greater impact from reducing inequalities than from spending more on health services or lifestyle changes.

The proposals are:

- **A progressive system of taxation, benefits and pensions** to provide greater support for people at the lower end of the social gradient and do more to reduce inequalities in wealth.
- **Development and implementation of a minimum income for a healthy life**, including an increase in the minimum wage.
- **More resources to support vulnerable populations**, by providing better homeless services, mental health services and other social care.
- **More resources for active labour market programmes** to reduce long-term unemployment and for primary healthcare services in deprived areas.
- **An enhanced home building programme**, including for decent social housing, to bring down housing costs.
- **Reduced traffic speeds in urban areas**, starting with the poorest areas, especially to protect children and older people.
- **Increased social protection** (social security, welfare and labour market interventions) for those on the lowest incomes

and more flexible income and welfare support for those moving in and out of work.

- **An increased proportion of government expenditure allocated to the early years of life**, focused progressively across the income distribution.

# POLICY IDEA 4

# What's the best way of delivering social care?

*Jane Lethbridge*

## What's the issue?

How to provide adequate social care is a major issue facing the UK. Care services, both residential and home care, have been systematically privatised since 1991. The failures of privatised provision, aggravated by austerity inflicted on both social care budgets and the NHS, have landed the system in crisis. Almost everyone will need care at some time, in the same way that everyone requires NHS services. Yet, there is no National Care Service.

The solution requires not only providing enough care, but also developing new and different forms of care. People's expectations of living longer affect how they want care to be delivered. Increasingly, people want care delivered in a personalised way at home or locally in the community.

**How could a National Care Service solve the social care crisis?**

## Analysis

Although life expectancy has been increasing, with women expected to live for 82.9 years and men for 79.2 years, these extra years will not necessarily all be spent in good health; many people will develop long-term conditions, affecting their mobility and ability to live independently. Men can expect to live 79.7 per cent of their lives in good health, while for women, who experience higher levels of limiting long-term conditions, the percentage is just 77.1 per cent. These differences between life expectancy and healthy life expectancy fuel the growing demand for care support services.

Over the coming 20 years, the population aged 65–84 will rise by 39 per cent and that aged over 85 by 106 per cent. With a larger older population, the demand for services to provide care for those not in good health will increase.

Informal carers provide a large amount of care unpaid and largely unsupported. In 2010, there were 5.3 million informal carers in UK. By 2037, this is estimated to grow to 9 million. Informal carers need support to continue do their work; they require both money and services, including professional help with increasingly complex caring activities, most obviously when dealing with dementia.

By 2032 over 11 million people are expected to be living on their own, which will be more than 40 per cent of all households. They will not be able to depend on family or partners for informal care.

Recent political debates on how to pay for care provision have floundered on whether a new form of social insurance should be introduced to pay for care, or whether property-owning households should have to sell their assets to pay for care. Alternatively, the growing amount needed could come from increased taxation and/or savings on other expenditures, such as Trident.

## What can we do?

Any good care system should maximise the control people have over their lives. This principle implies designing care services that meet local and individual needs. These services should be publicly owned, publicly funded and publicly delivered, rather than provided for profit. A National Care Service would be centrally funded, but locally delivered and work in partnership with the NHS, driven by the needs of local people rather than the shareholders and investors controlling for-profit providers. It would focus on improving:

- **Delivery.** Local authorities are best placed to deliver care services, using local democratic, participatory structures to involve local people and in-house services to design and deliver community-based services. Existing for-profit providers would be taken over by the public sector. Not-for-profit providers would be encouraged to develop innovative ways of delivering care.
- **Funding.** A National Care Service should deliver care free at the point of access and be funded through taxation. Any use of household assets to pay for care services should occur collectively and be paid through the taxation system, for example, through changes to inheritance taxes.
- **Care workforce.** Care workers should be well trained, well paid and supported in their work. In order make care work a more valued and higher-status profession, a new system of vocational education would be introduced to encourage younger people to consider care service as a career. There would be continuous professional development for existing paid care workers, and older people and unpaid carers who wanted to become formal, paid care workers would receive (re)training.
- **Attitudes to care.** Currently society does not sufficiently recognise the importance of care work. In order to build a National Care Service, attitudes towards older people and people with disabilities will need to become more positive, so that sensitive, appropriate and well-funded care services are seen as central to a progressive society.

## POLICY IDEA 5

# How do we make drug prices an easier pill for the NHS to swallow?

*Dean Baker*

**What's the issue?**

The pharmaceutical industry is charging ever-higher prices for its drugs, making them unaffordable for individuals and public healthcare systems. While the UK NHS, unlike the US government, negotiates drug prices with manufacturers, there have been some instances where it has been unable to reach an agreement on providing potentially lifesaving drugs to patients in the UK. Even the negotiated prices are rising rapidly, taking up an ever-larger share of the NHS' budget.

What policy should a progressive government implement to reduce the burden on the NHS of overall expenditure on drugs without the rationing of drugs threatening the nation's health?

## Analysis

It is government policy, not market processes, which cause high drug prices. Government legislation grants patent monopolies that have the negative effects that free market-oriented economists typically ascribe to government interference in the market. Altering government policy on patents would make drugs cheaper for the NHS, and thus increase provision.

Governments grant patent monopolies to provide an incentive for research and development of new drugs. The same purpose could be achieved by governments funding research directly, either carried directly within the public sector (for example, in the NHS or universities) or contracted out to private companies, including those that now do patent-supported research.

Public funding would allow patents to be placed in the public domain, facilitating the production of generic drugs. Such open access to patent rights would be restricted to the UK and countries with which there are reciprocal agreements. The UK government would derive revenue from patent rights in other countries. In almost all cases this approach would result in drugs being available to the NHS at a low cost, because few drugs are expensive to manufacture. Patents and other government-granted monopolies make drugs expensive, not the cost of producing them.

In addition to the savings from having drugs sold as generics, there would also be the benefit to public health resulting from full and open information about the safety and effectiveness of the drug. Patents give drug companies an incentive to misrepresent the effectiveness of their drugs and to conceal evidence that is harmful to patients.

If the UK government financed research, they could insist that all findings be made fully public. This would include the results of all clinical trials (subject to confidentiality restrictions), allowing physicians and other researchers to determine the best drug for specific patients. For example, some drugs may prove more effective for women than men, or older people than younger, or lead to negative reactions for people with specific conditions. Making clinical trial results fully public would lead to better prescribing decisions and better directed research on future drugs.

In a context in which the UK government alone provides direct public research funding it could act like a drug company in marketing its drugs overseas. It could set prices comparable to what other drug companies charge for their drugs, or consciously drive down prices. Marketing and negotiation could be contracted out to private companies, initially at least will have greater expertise, under strict policy guidelines.

Even a small number of new drugs made available at generic prices would be an incredibly powerful example. At modest cost the NHS could have state-of-the-art drugs for treating cancer, AIDS and other deadly diseases. This would generate pressure to have all drugs financed publicly. Also, making the data from clinical trials fully open to the public will be a powerful precedent that could force the pharmaceutical industry to do the same.

Patents and other forms of intellectual property have been a major factor in the growing inequality of incomes of the last four decades. If alternatives to patents can be developed in the pharmaceutical industry, they may be applied to other sectors. If more progressive mechanisms can be developed to promote research and creative work, it could contribute toward reversing the rise in inequality.

## What can we do?

- **The NHS should buy the rights to promising drugs at the pre-clinical phase and pay for the clinical trials**. It could also buy the rights to drugs at the first stage of clinical testing and pay for the larger and costlier phase II and phase III trials. If these trials proved successful, new drugs could be on the market at generic prices in five to ten years after the testing has begun.
- While there is considerable dispute about the cost of clinical trials, it is likely that the average cost for clinical trials for a successful drug would be about £100 million. The savings and profits from other countries could easily dwarf these costs and the funds invested in purchasing the rights to the drug. The savings would be from the new drug sold as

a generic, as well as the price reduction impact on other drugs; the profits would arise from selling drugs and patent rights abroad.

- **Alternatively, the UK government could adopt a 'copyleft' policy on the patents from its research** whereby others are free to use the findings, as long as any subsequent patents were themselves subject to copyleft restrictions. They would be fully open to any manufacturer that did not seek to patent an innovation in restriction of general access.

# POLICY IDEA 6

# How much would high-quality childcare cost and how would we pay for it?

*Jerome De Henau*

## What's the issue?

Although few governments of industrialised countries provide universal childcare, most recognise that accessible and affordable provision of high-quality pre-school childcare is an investment in the future wellbeing of children as well as a way to increase (women's) employment.

UK childcare policy represents the failure of state-subsidised market-based provision, with parents being charged some of the highest fees in the world and a marked socioeconomic gradient in accessibility and quality of provision. Yet, investing public money to provide universal high-quality childcare is not only beneficial socially; it also has fiscal advantages due to creating large employment effects on both the demand and supply side.

> What are the real costs of providing free universal high-quality childcare, and how can it be paid for?

## Analysis

The childcare system in the UK is totally inadequate. Because of the public good nature of childcare – a service whose benefits reach beyond its direct users – relying on private funding is insufficient. Unless the government pays for those additional benefits to society, no one funds them, and childcare is under-provided. This means government intervention is required to sustain childcare provision at an optimal level.

However, over the last 20 years, increased government investment in the sector – through a complex combination of cash subsidies to low-income working parents, tax breaks and direct support to providers – has failed to tackle the issues of quality, accessibility and affordability. Quality remains poor, mainly due to low pay and qualifications, despite strict staffing ratios being required.

Access is highly unequal, too. In 2009, under-three-year-olds in the 20 per cent highest-income families were six times more likely than those in the bottom 20 per cent to be in formal childcare in the UK, compared to 1.5 more likely in Germany, Belgium and Italy, and 1.2 in Denmark and Sweden. And, since then, austerity cuts have made childcare support to low-income families even less generous.

The government also funds direct subsidies to providers for the entitlement to 15 hours of free childcare (early years education) for all three- and four-year-olds (and, more recently, an additional 15 hours for those with parents in employment), with slight variations across the four nations of the UK. Most observers agree that the level of subsidy is too low, below running costs, despite the staff being poorly paid and qualification levels often inadequate, with only 14 per cent of childcare staff having a degree and qualified staff paid about 50 per cent less than their primary school teacher counterparts with the same level of qualification. Moreover, childcare is only available during the school term.

The UK government has pledged to spend about £6 billion a year on childcare by 2020, £1 billion more than in 2015. However, this would simply keep childcare spending broadly constant as a share of GDP, at just below 0.3 per cent, well below the OECD (Organisation for Economic Co-operation and Development) average of 0.7 per cent. This low spending reflects the UK's low level of provision, qualifications and pay compared to other European countries.

Despite inadequate services and uneven take-up, on average UK children are enrolled at rates similar to other European countries, around 30 per cent for those under the age of three and more than 80 per cent for those aged four and above. But, unlike in most other countries (except Ireland and the Netherlands), take-up in the UK is mostly part-time, with an average weekly enrolment of 14 hours for under-threes and 21 hours for older children, well below the European average of more than 30 hours.

As a result, childcare is largely informal, provided mostly by mothers and grandmothers, with long-term detrimental consequences for women's economic independence. But, more importantly, children start their life with very unequal chances and prospects for wellbeing. Indeed, there is overwhelming evidence that high-quality full-time childcare targeted at disadvantaged children improves their social skills and wellbeing, and helps reduce the gap in their school achievements compared with their wealthier peers. Universal schemes have also been shown to result in better social and academic outcomes for all children (and more so for disadvantaged ones), but only if the childcare is of high quality, which requires not just well-paid, trained staff but also sufficient time spent interacting with children to nurture healthy and flourishing relationships.

**What can we do?**

A national education system, free at the point of use, should include early years, with universal high-quality childcare provided at sufficient scale to meet needs. Therefore, a system with the following characteristics is proposed:

- **Universal.** Every child would be entitled to a full-time place from an early age, say, six months, until they enter primary school.

- **Affordable.** Places should be free at the point of use, as they are in schools, to encourage take-up by those who would benefit most.
- **High quality.** Well-qualified staff (45 per cent with a university degree), reasonable child/staff ratios, good pay (on primary school pay scales, including a public sector pension). This also requires safe and welcoming premises with sufficient indoor and outdoor space for playing, sleeping, eating, etc.

Several scenarios with different levels of generosity, and thus quality, are simulated in my working paper *Employment and Fiscal Effects of Investing in Universal Childcare* (De Henau, 2019) (all costings in 2014 prices):

- Extending provision at current quality standards (child/staff ratios, pay and qualifications) to all pre-school children would cost about £32 billion per year, or 1.7 per cent of GDP. Increasing qualification levels (to 45 per cent of staff having a degree) at current pay scales would make the total cost £35 billion per year, or 1.9 per cent of GDP.
- The most generous scenario of increasing qualifications and paying childcare staff on primary school pay scales would require an annual gross investment of £57 billion, or 3.1 per cent of GDP.

All scenarios include funding for building new facilities and training staff to required qualification levels.

The gross cost of any of these scenarios is far more than the £5 billion per year spent by the government in 2015 on childcare subsidies. However, making this additional annual spending fiscally 'affordable' does not require fully funding it by an increase in tax rates, because the spending on childcare would itself generate additional tax revenue. We can estimate this in two ways. One way is as the additional tax revenue stemming from increased employment created in the economy, and the other is as the additional tax paid by mothers increasing their lifelong earning gains through improved employment prospects.

A generous system of universal childcare would result in significant employment creation, not just directly in the childcare sector, but also due to indirect and induced employment effects. Indirect employment would be created in industries supplying the inputs needed to provide childcare: food, electricity, buildings, training etc. Induced employment would be generated by newly employed workers, both in childcare and those indirectly employed, spending their earnings.

In the most generous childcare scenario listed above, the total employment created would be about 1.7 million full-time equivalent jobs, one-third of which would be outside the childcare sector. This is a rise of four percentage points in the employment rate. Assuming gender segregation remains unchanged, women's employment rate would rise by 6.5 percentage points and the gender employment gap would halve.

Increased employment would yield increased revenue from tax on both income and expenditure, as well as reduced social security payments to those who are newly employed. The net additional annual funding required would be only about a quarter of the gross investment, taking account of existing spending on childcare. This means about three-quarters of the gross annual funding would be recouped on a year-on-year basis.

Another way of looking at the additional tax revenue generated is through the improved lifetime employment prospects of the mothers who, with childcare, can remain in employment when their children are small. If the employment penalty that mothers face after the birth of their first child over their working life can be avoided through the provision of high-quality childcare, then the tax revenue accumulated from the 'regained' (that is, not lost) earnings should be set against the costs to the state of that childcare. Childcare provision is 'fiscally affordable' in the narrow sense of the term (that is, breaking even), once a mother has worked a sufficient number of years that the tax revenue from her 'regained' earnings has paid for the childcare for her children. In the most generous childcare scenario, for a typical mother of two children earning wages free of any child-related penalty, it takes about 12 to 15 years for the government to recoup in taxes the cost of her children's childcare, well within the usual working lifespan of most mothers.

# POLICY IDEA 7

# What should be done about private schools?

*Francis Green and David Kynaston*

## What's the issue?

For all the talk of grammar schools, academies and free schools, the British school system remains dominated by a small but powerful segment at its summit – its private schools. Until some radical reform is set in train, an unreconstructed private school system, with its current enormous resource superiority and exclusiveness, hanging over the state system as a beacon for unequal treatment and privilege, will make it impossible to sustain a fair and socially just state education system. The reform of private schools should be a priority.

> How can private schools be reformed to make the school system better and fairer for all?

## Analysis

Britain's private schools provide a good education for their pupils in several ways. But they hold back the children educated in state schools. They secure a hugely disproportionate share of places at Oxford, Cambridge and other prestigious universities, and offer a golden ticket to financially rewarding jobs. They help to perpetuate a low level of social mobility. Above all, this is unfair, and the majority feel this way: in a recent poll, more than three-quarters of those who expressed an opinion one way or the other agreed that private schooling in the UK is unfair. Moreover, the concentration of our teaching resources on just this small segment of the population is socially inefficient. And the hold of the privately educated on positions of influence is deeply undemocratic.

Private schooling has become a sophisticated service industry, much changed from the spartan settings of half a century ago. Since the 1980s, resources have ballooned, and fees have trebled in real terms, the average now standing at over £17,000 per year for one child. Management has been modernised. Several studies show that private schools are associated with better academic progress at every educational stage through to sixth form. This evidence is based on comparisons that control for children's social and economic backgrounds, and for their prior achievements. Private schools are more effective at preparing children for conventional exams; they also deliver a broader educational curriculum than is afforded in state schools, with much emphasis on cultural and sporting activities. Their successes owe much to their vastly superior resources, and the concentration within them of a peer group having relatively few social and behavioural problems. There are now twice as many teachers per pupil in the private sector, and the private/state gap in support staff, facilities and wealth is even greater.

Private school alumni do not do quite so well once at university, but the gains made up to that point are enough to ensure that the privately educated enter their careers with much-enhanced educational qualifications. On top of that, the schools offer as part of the package 'social and cultural capital' – superior networks, advice and guidance on careers and university choices. Little surprise, then, that the privately educated gain disproportionate access to high-status occupations, including in the creative industries and the arts, and obtain a substantial earnings premium. The schools' traditional disproportionate influence in political life persists shockingly in the 21st century.

Yet the schools do not need to be so expensive in order to be good schools. The reason their fees are so high is not to do with illegal cartel pricing (even if some schools were sanctioned in 2006 following a minor price-fixing scandal). Nor is it a tactical mistake, as some have suggested. The fees are primarily set high as an excluding device, to limit the social composition of their pupils to the affluent, with just a few exceptions for especially able children from poor families. The high fees enable schools to provide a level of luxury that would, perhaps, be normal at home for many of the children they take, but would astonish those from ordinary backgrounds.

## What can we do?

A progressive strategy for education and society needs to **reform the UK's private school system**, rather than ignore it. Its relatively small size in terms of pupil numbers, 7 per cent, belies the resources consumed and the sector's influence in society. Of course, there are many other issues to be addressed in the UK's schools, and in the household and general living environments where children learn and develop their capacities. But these other issues are not substitutes for tackling the private school problem. That is why radical private school reform is not only necessary, but should become a priority. There needs to be a national conversation on this topic.

It is not an option simply to hope that private schools will wither away. Politicians have wished for this on past occasions – in vain. Moreover, studies of parental choice show that persuading parents to shun private schooling for their own children if they think that the system is unfair will not work. We cannot hope to reduce the demand this way. An inclusive policy is needed that recognises opportunities missed by past politicians and avoids their mistakes.

Current government policy is to use the private schools to improve state schools. Debate on how far the schools are already doing this, and whether the threat of removal of charitable status should be used to induce deeper 'partnerships', barely touches the basic problems of the system. The current Labour Party policy in opposition is to charge VAT on school fees, which would raise some £2 billion pounds to spend on free school meals for all. (A more flexible plan is simply to add this sum to the education budget.) Essentially, this is a more aggressive and punitive strategy than the government's to achieve the same aim: improving state schools. Estimates of price elasticity suggest that perhaps 30,000 children would then switch to state schools, reducing the net gain in state revenues by a small amount. Yet, with a population of more than half a million children, the private school system would survive, only a little smaller than before.

A more radical and effective policy would aim to reform the whole system, to **remove progressively the private/state divide**. There are two ways of going about this. First, one could, in addition to taxing school fees, reduce still further the demand for private schooling, aiming to force their closure as private bodies. Mandating that universities use 'contextual' admissions that favour state school children over private school children would be one way to reduce the demand for private education, by lowering its perceived benefits.

A second approach is to **enforce a partial integration of private schools with the state education system**. This solution – far from abolition – would directly preserve the excellence of many private schools, while harnessing what they have to offer more equitably and effectively. In the 'Fair Access Scheme' that David Kynaston and I have proposed, all private schools would be obliged to admit a third of pupils from low-income families. The state would pay schools at the same per capita rate that they fund state school pupils, and the schools would be regulated to ensure that the state-funded pupils were fully integrated and treated in the same way as fee-paying pupils. Importantly, the state (whether central, regional or local) must exercise full control over admissions codes. In effect the state-funded places at private schools would become an outsourced part of the state education system.

The schools would have to adapt over the first few years to the more socially mixed clientele, as each successive cohort of children becomes part-composed of state-funded pupils, and they would face a difference between the funds received from the government for the state-funded students and their current, pre-reform, costs. The schools would have to retrench considerably, some more than others, incrementally removing some of the schools' luxuries, taking advantage of their current costs being far higher than are necessary to provide a good education. They would be able to devote their accumulated funds, previously used for bursaries and scholarships, to meeting some of their income shortfall. Beyond that, fees would rise for fee-paying families, leading some parents to switch their children away from the private sector and into their local state schools; others might leave because the exclusivity for which they were previously paying would no longer be provided. A minority of private schools would close or become state schools.

Such a reform will call on a determined political will, since the autonomy of private schools will be partly undermined, and entrenched interests would be brought to bear in their defence. Earlier campaigns for private school reform were put off in part by the excuse that the money in the education budget was too scarce. Yet a policy such as the **Fair Access Scheme** would not require an enormous increase in the nation's education budget, which must, anyway, expand to provide new places for our expanding population. It would be a feasible start in bringing the nation's children together.

## POLICY IDEA 8

# How do we make lifelong learning a reality for all?

*Liz Marr*

**What's the issue?**

Despite much talk about the importance of lifelong learning, the UK has never had any universal 'cradle to grave' education policy. Instead, it has been assumed that addressing skills sector by sector through industrial strategy will suffice.

Within higher education, the sole focus has been on the provision of the traditional face-to-face boarding school university for 18-year-olds. Policy to widen access has concentrated on getting bright young people from poor backgrounds into elite institutions, while opportunities for mature students to study part time have declined.

This is in part due to lack of funding, but also to the dysfunctional structure of the higher and further education sector, a result of it being viewed by policy-makers as a quasi-market. Indeed, Peter Scott, Commissioner for Fair Access in Scotland, contends that policy-makers view lifelong learning with incomprehension and condescension.

What policies would be effective in reversing the decline in adult part-time study in post-compulsory education?

## Analysis

The future working life of young people, both those in the labour market today and those still to enter it, will be very different to that of their parents and grandparents. They will be employed for longer, perhaps in the 'gig' economy, and may have portfolio careers with frequent need to learn new skills and move between sectors. Increasingly rapid changes in technology are transforming the world of work in a global context, closing down some industries but creating new ones at the same time.

Universities will have to look at how to remain relevant, how to ensure that students are prepared for industries that we don't yet know will exist, and how to continue to support those same learners throughout their lives. Existing policy does not and cannot address the flexibility needed for universities to do this because it positions higher education as a private good, placing the burden of funding on students and treating higher education as a market. Policy-makers seem to forget that education is a public good too, benefiting society as a whole as well as its direct 'consumers'.

Higher education certainly does allocate such a private 'good' to some people, in the form of higher lifetime earnings and subsidiary benefits of improved health and wellbeing, for graduates and their families. But note that such allocations are inevitably skewed towards those who have had advantages in accessing higher education by dint of family background, schooling and other elements of cultural and economic capital. Current policy on widening access and participation in higher education still privileges the idea that some universities are better than others and that poor, bright kids should aspire to these.

The hierarchical nature of the higher education and qualification frameworks also privileges academic over vocational awards (except in those more highly paid disciplines like law or medicine). Young people are made to choose very early on in their schooling between studying academic or vocational courses, often directed to one or the other according to their social background, reinforcing class distinctions.

The public good of higher education is more evenly spread – universities prepare doctors, teachers, engineers, lawyers, economists and artists, and we all benefit from their contributions to society through their professional expertise, research, enterprise and knowledge exchange.

Nonetheless, the funding of higher education remains contentious, having moved from grants made directly to institutions to indirect funding through student loans to pay fees. This was based on the belief that those who benefit directly – both students and business – should pay. In 2012, lifting the fee cap to £9,000 (now £9,250) made higher education in England very expensive. The stipulation that only those registered for a full qualification, such as a diploma or a bachelor's degree, would be eligible for loan funding had a drastic impact on part-time study, and especially on those who wished to study for a small amount of credit, in order to meet a skills need at work, for example.

Between 2008/09 and 2016/17, the decline in part-time higher education numbers has been dramatic in the UK, falling by 47.5 per cent, but even more marked in England, with the fall hitting 53 per cent. The majority of the reduction has occurred in what are termed 'other undergraduate' courses, mainly at sub-degree level, and thus generally in more vocational subjects. The decline has mainly been attributed to economic factors, specifically the increase in tuition fees.

A no less significant factor was denying loans to those wishing to study for an equivalent or lower qualification to one they already had. Thus individuals who had already been funded for a degree in history, for example, were not eligible for a loan to retrain in engineering or computing science, although some restrictions in loans for studying strategically important disciplines such as science, technology, engineering and maths (STEM) have now been lifted. However, higher education funding remains dominated by the aim of making an individual pay for the acquisition of a private good rather than ensuring the benefit to the community of the public good of having an adaptive education system that allows reskilling to meet the needs of a changing economy.

Current policy discourse in England does make reference to social justice and social mobility but overlooks the fact that these terms are *not* mutually interchangeable. Widening access to higher education may be a form of social justice in giving people greater equality of opportunity, but does not necessarily result in social mobility by delivering equal outcomes in the form of better employment options.

There is growing awareness that traditional qualifications are not ideal for those lifelong learners seeking smaller targeted but rigorous learning at higher education level, which can be studied flexibly and online. The introduction of recognised micro-credentials could address national skills gaps. The New Zealand Qualifications Authority, seeing this potential, is funding its universities to produce micro-credentials as part of their formal higher education framework. At a European level there is interest in the idea of Short Learning Programmes (SLPs) as stand-alone elements of networked qualifications. An SLP is a short programme, focused on specific social economic needs, delivered flexibly (online) and at scale and accredited.

In the UK, unlike other European countries, such programmes exist in the form of certificates of higher education, but these take a whole year of full-time study, and there is currently nothing smaller that can be funded outside an existing formal qualification structure. However, universities need to be incentivised to see smaller qualifications as worthwhile elements of a qualification framework and to be more willing to recognise credit awarded by other providers in a much more networked approach.

## What can we do?

The need to retrain, update skills or change career direction will be essential as technologies and markets change and develop increasingly rapidly. Adults already in employment, or displaced from defunct sectors, will need to study flexibly and in new and different ways. This will require new models of delivery, wider recognition of what counts as academic credentials and funding schemes that incentivise rather than deter participation.

The following elements are proposed as essential components of an effective policy for lifelong learning, with a specific focus on higher education:

- **Loans** should be available for single modules at any size/study intensity without commitment to a minimum qualification level.
- **Credit** should be fully portable between institutions, nationally and internationally, and provision should be 'stackable' such that networked qualifications become possible. In other words, a learner should be able to study at different institutions throughout their lives and collect credit to make a full certificate or degree.
- **Qualification frameworks** should be aligned so that learners can move freely between the further and higher education sectors, accumulating both academic and vocational credit as and when needed.
- **Smaller credit sizes** should be recognised as formal credentials by government agencies, which should encourage employers to consider them alongside more well-known qualifications.
- People should have **lifetime learning accounts** so that they can take up regular re- or up-skilling, and spread their learning across their life.
- Institutions should be incentivised to make more **part-time and flexible provision** available, with a particular focus on the use of technologies to increase accessibility and inclusion.
- Employers should be able to use the **apprenticeship levy** for all forms of accredited training and continuing professional development (CPD) for their staff, including short courses and employer-based training, for example.

# Conclusion

*Jeremy Smith*

We have sought to organise the policy proposals in this book under five broad themes that reflect principles of a future-focused social democracy. However, the ideas set out here come from almost 40 authors, and – despite their breadth and scope – neither pretend nor aim to form a comprehensive package of social and economic policy proposals.

Moreover, one of our editorial purposes for this book is to encourage and facilitate readers to dip in and out of the contributions, according to interest and opportunity. We have therefore not sought to set out a definitive set of 'conclusions' that would claim to draw together all the strands of policy to be found within the book's cover.

What unites all the contributions, however, is a spirit – a clear, strong sense that the hitherto dominant economic paradigm is not only shifting but also melting before our eyes, and that new policy solutions are urgently needed.

Since 1945, the UK and indeed all those countries comprising the 'advanced economies' have lived through two discrete politico-economic eras, each lasting some 30 years, and each giving rise to its specific suite of social and economic policies.

The first, which lasted (more or less) till the late 1970s, and whose end was symbolised by the British government going to the International Monetary Fund (IMF) for a 'structural adjustment' programme, we may call the era of managed capitalism, with a mixed economy and strong welfare state, and full employment as a key goal. Despite its hard ending, this era saw bigger increases in GDP per head and incomes, and lower inequality, than in any other.

The second, the 'free market' age, in which the state promoted and enforced liberalisation, privatisation and financial deregulation, held sway until the global financial crisis struck in 2008. The argument (often self-interested) that deregulated globalised finance, leading as it did to the build-up of unprecedented levels of private debt, was for the public benefit, imploded almost overnight amid its own contradictions, along with the economy itself.

Until 2007, GDP per head on average continued to rise at a reasonably fast rate (2.3 to 2.4 per cent average per year). Inequality rose sharply, as measured by the UK Gini coefficient, between 1979 and 1991 (from 0.26 to 0.34), before plateauing a little below the 1991 level. Annual GDP per head almost stalled for over a decade (the average change from 2008 to 2017 being just 0.4 per cent). No other decade since 1945 has seen such a weak overall economic development. The fact that unemployment fell back from a crisis peak of over 8 per cent in 2011 to its lowest levels since the early 1970s is simply another way of describing the 'productivity puzzle' – paradoxically, while technological change appeared to accelerate, the rate of productivity change has markedly declined.

There should be no doubt that austerity – even if the UK model was slightly less extreme than that imposed on or practised by some Eurozone countries – contributed to this economically dismal decade. Not only did it act as a fiscal 'drag' on the economy – by focusing on cuts in public services (as well as in benefits) it lowered the social wage, affecting the poor and women disproportionately – while changes and reductions in taxation ensured that the better-off were far less affected, and maintained their power to privately consume. Since poorer people tend to rely more on public services for their wellbeing, this has had the effect of increasing actual social inequality. And, while racism has always existed, the growing economic and social divisions (mirrored also in regional divergences) have surely helped to stoke its fires and target some of the 'blame' for our plight on to migrants and, more generally, the 'other'.

The economic historian Karl Polanyi, writing in 1940, argued, in a section headed 'National boundaries as shock-absorbers', that:

> If international division of labour is effected by competition and consequent elimination of the less efficient, then much will depend upon the rate at which the change proceeds as well as upon the dimensions of the units involved....While a slowly increasing division of labour effected by the market mechanism would be purely beneficial, a fast rate of change might work out as a machinery of sheer destruction. (From Smith, 2017)

In his view, 'Modern nationalism is a protective reaction against the dangers inherent in an interdependent world'. But that protective reaction could be positive (the state moving in a democratic direction) or negative (a turn to authoritarianism).

Fast forward to the present age of financial globalisation, and the pace of change imposed by its relentless algorithms can be seen as operating – for some – as just such a 'machinery of destruction'.

Which brings us back to Britain and the intense divisions experienced over Brexit. There is a strong sense – and Brexit may be seen as a potent symbol or harbinger – that we are on the cusp of a new and very different era, but one whose philosophical as well as political outcome remains to be determined.

Will we see a further political shift towards right-wing nationalism in Britain, reflecting the 'strong man' authoritarian trends in other parts of the world? In this scenario, the policy ideas in this book will surely be destined to lie untested and unconsidered, quietly gathering dust.

But there is the alternative, optimistic future on which this book is premised, and for which it is destined. In this scenario, the nation-state plays a positive role in providing society with security, protection and redistribution, to counter the destructive excesses of the global market and financial systems. We imagine

— anticipate — a new, progressive government taking office, dedicated to tackling inequality and to addressing the challenges.

As history tells us, a government committed to restructuring power relationships must know in advance what it will do, and needs to be ready to act. Take the example of Roosevelt's first presidency, when in his first days and months in office in 1933 he handled the banking crisis, took on the power of finance, released the US from the gold standard and instituted a giant programme of public works. And this was just the start — but a start without which the rest of the New Deal programme would not have been possible. It reframed the sense of what was politically possible, and reconfigured — not wholly but significantly — the overall power relationship with Wall Street.

Our modest purpose through this brief book is to help make such a radical, democratic and popular programme feasible: to stimulate a broader, more radical policy debate, to offer a diverse menu of robust, progressive policy ideas.

At the core of any transformative programme must be macroeconomic policy. Until now, the traditional Treasury orthodoxy — enthusiastically supported for their own political reasons by recent governments — has given unyielding intellectual support to austerity as economic policy. Sir Nicholas (now Lord) Macpherson, former Permanent Secretary to the Treasury, in 2016 described Chancellor Osborne's policies as 'perfectly sensible'. He added: 'I've only had four years in 31 at the Treasury when there has been a surplus. If you don't aim to get the surplus, you'll never get there.' Yet Sir Nicholas was candid enough also to say:

> I see myself as one of a number of people in finance ministries, central bank regulators, in the UK and the US who failed to see the crisis coming, who failed to spot the build-up of risk.... This was a monumental collective intellectual error. (Parker, 2016)

Our contributors have (in Part One) rejected the Treasury orthodoxy — a future progressive government needs to start with a new macroeconomic paradigm. In headline terms, *the government is not like, or constrained in the same way as, a household.*

The economy's primary focus should be on good quality employment, making full use of the country's overall economic capacity, and on productive investment in our future (including social investment, and not least to address the great generational challenge of climate change), on tackling inequality, and on promoting equity both through taxation and public spending priorities.

In Parts Two and Three, our authors have addressed the linked issues of public investment, industrial strategy, rebalancing workplace rights, new ways of structuring and democratising corporations, and redirecting 'finance' to a more social role. The UK government has been resistant to the adoption of any of these policies. The UK is at the bottom of the public investment league for 'advanced' economies. We (as a nation) have refused to develop a serious, forward-looking modern industrial strategy. We have ignored the merits and successful examples of National Investment Banks in other countries. We have stripped workers of rights and protections, and allowed a low-pay economy to evolve. This is why the UK always comes near the top of the OECD's (Organisation for Economic Co-operation and Development) league table of 'labour market flexibility', and why real wages have been able to fall so dramatically.

In the neoliberal era of deregulated finance, 'finance' has become ever more disconnected from the productive economy and acted only in its own interest. But 'finance' should not be seen as always and inevitably an enemy. The task is to harness and channel it, for productive purposes for the common good.

In our final parts, Four and Five, looking at what makes for genuine social security and at providing for social needs, our authors have proposed new ways to tackle some of our sharpest, and most urgent, social issues. Our market-obsessed society has offered little or no help or protection from exploitation for those forced or lured into debt, to rent sub-standard housing, or to cash in their pension pots. For those needing to apply for state benefits, the present system, worsened in practice with the flawed roll-out of Universal Credit, has proved harsh and error-prone. And then there are the great but fragile community services – health, care services, education, housing and so on – whose public quality has been undermined by austerity and/or dogmatic and often poorly performing privatisation, or which risk sliding into decay as needs and resources move further apart.

Not least in these parts of the book we start to pose some deep questions about the policy dilemmas for our society as technological change permeates ever more deeply. Will 'work' and 'employment' continue to be seen as essential not only to our economic life but also to our sense of purpose as humans? Will society need as many 'workers' as hitherto? Our contributors differ as to the answers, but can surely agree that we will need, whether via paid employment or otherwise, to dedicate more of our time and 'human resources' on caring for each other and for the planet, and learning how better to do so. Universal Basic Income is one response to this question.

We have recalled, above, FDR's first days in office, in which his programme of radical reform was firmly installed, and for which strong public support was generated and enlisted. In the UK, the 1945 Labour government is sometimes seen as having a near equivalent impact, with its introduction of the National Health Service, the wider welfare state, a broad commitment to full employment, and the 'nationalisation' of the Bank of England. Clement Attlee was both more cautious than FDR, and in an even more complex situation; the war still continued for several weeks in the East, and the burden of reconstruction and external war debts imposed from the outset harsh economic constraints.

Today, we face huge challenges and risks as a country, and fundamental choices of political and economic direction. Our situation is not so grave as in 1945, for sure, but the choices we make now will shape our country for many decades to come.

We face, broadly, three choices for the UK's future. The first is of conservative nationalism. The second is of market fundamentalism. The third is a progressive turn to the values of social democracy, translated into policies shaped to support and liberate the many, not to empower and enrich the few.

# Jargon busters

**Accumulation** The acquisition of assets through their continuing growth.

**Allocative efficiency** Allocating resources in the most efficient way possible, so that without more resources it would not be possible to make anyone better off.

**Annuity** A bond that pays a guaranteed income for a specified period of time, for example, for its owner's lifetime. Lifetime annuities are often taken out by retirees to convert their accumulated pension funds into incomes.

**Arbitrage** Making use of a divergence of prices in two markets, to buy an asset in one market and sell it in another market at a higher price. Such arbitrage tends to keep prices the same across different markets. Or selecting the most suitable choice from a range of possibilities. For example, for its head office, a bank or financial institution might select London over Frankfurt for its looser regulation, while a corporation might select Ireland over the UK for its more favourable tax regulations.

**Asset** Anything from which its owner can make money.

**Austerity** Reducing government spending and/or increasing taxes, usually in the hope of reducing the public deficit and debt (see **fiscal consolidation**).

**Automatic stabilisers** Taxes and social security benefit payments that stabilise the budget and day-to-day running of both the government and households across the economic cycle. During a boom, government tax income increases, while benefit payments are lower, and during a recession this situation reverses. They are 'automatic' because they don't require a change in legislation.

**Autonomy** Being able to make decisions without reference to others.

**Balanced budget** A government budget where income exactly balances spending, with neither a deficit nor a surplus.

**Bank (commercial)** A private sector bank that provides loans and other banking services to businesses and households. It may be part of a larger banking group.

**Bank (investment)** Originally, a bank that acts as an intermediary between investors and businesses that want either to raise funds by issuing shares or to sell the entire company. They also carry out other, higher-risk forms of investment. Although they technically don't hold customer deposits, they may well be part of a banking organisation that does.

**Bank (retail)** Banks that most of us use for our day-to-day money management. But, except for one of the few remaining Mutual Societies, these are generally part of a bank that also provides commercial and investment services in other divisions.

**Bank for International Settlements** An international financial regulator, based in Switzerland, that designs international regulation. It is run by government appointees from the largest capitalist economies.

**Behavioural effects** Changes in the behaviour of people in response to other changes, for example, in policies. Thus a behavioural effect of a rise in tobacco tax may be a reduction in smoking.

**Boom** Also termed 'expansion' or 'recovery'. The growth phase of the economic cycle – in other words, the opposite of a recession. It will involve strong GDP growth, however, as opposed to a recovery, where almost any amount of growth will do (see also **expansion**).

**Bubble** A bubble is the inflation of an asset price, such as shares of stock or houses, way beyond their sustainable value. It occurs through people believing that the price will continue to rise. The inevitable result is that sooner or later there will be a sudden readjustment to a much lower price when confidence that the price will continue rising fails and the bubble bursts.

**Budget deficit** If a government spends more during its financial year than it receives in taxes, the difference is called the budget deficit – and the government will have to borrow (or issue) money to cover it.

**Budget surplus** If the government spends less than it receives in tax income and asset sales, it will have money left over – a surplus.

**Business cycle** Also termed 'economic cycle' – the sequence of recessions and expansions in the economy.

**Capital** A firm's assets, including its fixed capital (machinery, buildings and so on), working capital (stocks of raw materials and half-finished products) and financial capital (money and other financial assets).

**Capital account** The part of the government's budget for spending on investment, which is likely to pay for itself over the longer term through increased tax income or user fees.

**Capital adequacy** A requirement that a private bank retains a certain minimum level of capital, its capital reserves, in relation to its assets. Such a banking regulation hopes to ensure that banks have enough internal financial resources (including shareholders' funds) to cope with unexpected drops in profitability.

**Capital flight** When investors (both foreign and domestic) abruptly withdraw their money from a country due to a sudden perceived risk, which could be economic, financial or political. Capital flight can cause depreciation of the national currency, shortage of credit and a rapid tightening of credit conditions that can lead to further falls in investment.

**Capitalism** An economic and political system, based on class divisions, where most economic activity is carried out by private (for-profit) businesses employing wage labour.

**Capital market liquidity** A measure of the ability of the market to provide enough money to maintain existing businesses, fund new ones and to keep money flowing – hence 'liquid' capital. The 2007 'Credit Crunch' – a shortage of credit – was the result of capital markets being 'illiquid' – basically frozen.

**Central Bank** A financial institution, usually controlled to some degree by the national government. 'Independent' central banks, like the Bank of England, can set short-term interest rates (theoretically, at least), without interference from politicians. The Bank of England lends to commercial banks and the government, and has, over the years, had varying degrees of responsibility for regulating private banks and other financial institutions.

**Citizen's wealth fund** While sovereign wealth funds, hedge funds, private equity and mutual funds all operate for the benefit of particular groups of people, a citizens' wealth fund is designed to benefit a country's citizens generally. The fund may be invested to provide financial payments to citizens, but is more likely used to provide improved infrastructure.

**Classical economics** The tradition of economics that began with Adam Smith, and continued with other theorists, including the likes of David Ricardo, Thomas Malthus and Jean-Baptiste Say. The classical economists wrote during the early years of capitalism, and they uniformly celebrated the productive, innovative actions of the new class of industrial capitalists. They focused on the dynamic economic and political development of capitalism, analysed economics in class terms, and often advocated a labour theory of value.

**Collective bargaining** A trade union bargaining with employers on behalf of its members over wages and conditions of employment.

**Consumer Price Index (CPI)** Measures changes in the *price* level of a basket of *consumer* goods and services purchased by households.

**Contraction** Also termed 'recession' or 'bust', although these three terms typically indicate an economic downturn of varying proportions. A contraction might mean a sudden slowing in GDP growth, perhaps with a quarter of negative GDP growth. By contrast, a recession is officially defined as two or more successive quarters of negative GDP growth, while a bust is more severe and usually involves a financial crisis of some sort and a degree of panic.

**Counter-cyclical policy** Designed to smooth out fluctuations in the economic cycle. It usually involves spending more during a recession, to support employment by investing in infrastructure, for example, and spending less during a boom, partly to stop the economy overheating and partly to build up resources to help in the next recession. Spending less during the recession, but more during the boom – pro-cyclical policy – will make booms and busts bigger.

**Credit crunch** A period when banks – which usually lend to clients and each other freely (see **capital market liquidity**) – stop lending. This is usually due to a loss of confidence or even a panic, often the result of a financial crisis. It can also be caused by financial institutions becoming insolvent. But, either way, there is an abrupt drop in available credit, which, in turn, can have dire consequences for both investment and consumption – reducing GDP growth and, unless there is government intervention, resulting in economic and social damage.

**Current account** The part of the government's budget for day-to-day spending and taxation, but not the spending that can be seen as an investment (**capital account**).

**Debt (national, public)** This is made up of all the annual budget deficits to date, including the interest on government borrowing and the cost of servicing them. If deficits continue and/or the cost of servicing existing debt rises, the national debt will also increase. However, a sustained budget surplus – usually the result of solid GDP growth (as opposed to austerity) – will reduce it.

**Debt-to-GDP ratio** The overall amount of debt a country has at any one moment, compared to the amount of its GDP.

**Deficit** When a government, business or household spends more in a given period of time than they receive in income and asset sales.

**Deindustrialisation** A shift in output and employment of a country or region away from manufacturing.

**Demand** The amount of a good or service that people are both willing and able to buy.

**Demand-led macroeconomic policy** Recognises that the amount that is produced in the economy depends on aggregate demand, the amount people, both consumers and investors, are willing to buy, and that increases in demand will generate increases in supply in response. Such policy is informed by Keynesian economics.

**Depression** No official definition, but an extreme version of a recession, which usually lasts years rather than quarters, and may well involve price deflation.

**Derivative** A financial asset whose value is 'derived' from bets on the value of other financial assets, which is why it can be highly unpredictable. Examples include the now notorious collateralised debt obligations (CDOs), whose difficulties of evaluation helped set off the 2008 financial crisis.

**Direct tax** See **tax (direct)**.

**Economic growth** An increase in GDP, adjusted for inflation, and so able to be compared over time and across countries.

**Economies of scale** Occur when the average cost of each unit produced falls the more is produced. This happens in industries where there are start-up costs and fixed assets, such as land and machinery, whose costs remain the same however much is produced.

**Employment and Support Allowance (ESA)** An income-replacement benefit for adults below state pension age who are having difficulty finding employment because of long-term medical conditions or a disability. ESA is currently being phased out and replaced with Universal Credit.

**Equity** The amount of an asset owned, after deducting any money borrowed to own it. Shares in firms are also known as equities.

**Exchange rate** The 'price' at which one country's currency can be converted into that of another country. Although a currency is called 'strong' if its exchange rate is 'high', this is not necessarily good news, because, although a country with a strong currency can pay for imports more easily and its citizens have more spending money on holiday abroad, it also makes exports more expensive and therefore less competitive.

**Expansion** A period of sustained GDP growth. The upward phase of the economic cycle – in other words, the opposite of a contraction. Also termed 'boom' or 'recovery'. A boom will involve strong GDP growth at the top of the cycle, while a recovery is any growth coming after a period of recession.

**Expansionary fiscal contraction** The idea that austerity – cutting government spending and/or raising taxes – can actually produce GDP growth in an economy mired in recession. Sadly, this is the economic equivalent of Big Foot: some economists claim to have seen it, but none have been able to prove it exists.

All the evidence shows that austerity in a recession will make things worse, not better.

**Expansionary policy** The opposite of austerity, increased government spending and/or reduced taxes, policies designed to promote employment, investment and GDP growth. For example, government investment in infrastructure, training and setting up special 'enterprise zones' would all be expansionary policies.

**Finance-led growth model** The idea that GDP growth can be promoted by developments in the financial sector, notably by reducing its transaction costs.

**Financial sector** Consists of firms that bring together those with money who want to invest with those who want to use funds to buy assets, and manages such transactions, also sometimes trading on their own behalf.

**Fiscal balance** The difference between a government's revenues (taxes and proceeds from asset sales) and its expenditures, often expressed as a ratio of gross domestic product (GDP). If the balance is positive, the government spends less than it receives and has a budget surplus. If the balance is negative, the government spends more than it receives and has a budget deficit.

**Fiscal consolidation** The idea behind austerity, reducing government deficit and debt.

**Financialisation** A process encouraged by neoliberalism's removal of tariff and capital flow barriers, where real production in the economy is accompanied – or even replaced – by rapidly growing financial activity, including speculation, lending, financial assets and securitisation and the appropriation of income in the form of rent. It has also brought a sharp increase in private debt levels, and in income inequalities. Its extent can be assessed by comparing the amount of purely financial assets in an economy to that of real capital assets.

**Fiscal multiplier** See **multiplier**.

**Fiscal policy** The means by which a government adjusts its spending levels and tax rates to monitor and influence a nation's economy.

**Fiscal rules** Fiscal rules impose constraints on fiscal policy through limits on how far government spending can deviate from its revenue.

**Floors and ceilings** Minimum (floor) and maximum (ceiling) amounts payable.

**Foreign direct investment** The acquisition or setting up of an operation overseas that includes fixed capital assets (such as buildings, machinery and equipment).

**Free market economy/policies** An economic system in which markets are allowed to operate with little or no government control. The belief that an economy functions best with least interference from government lay behind the free market policies of the Thatcher and Reagan governments of the 1980s.

**FTSE Index** A composite price index to show shifts in the value of UK-listed companies. These are not necessarily British companies; many are foreign, but quoted in London.

**Full employment** When everyone looking for work can quickly find a job, so unemployment is near zero.

**Generic drug** A drug that is effectively the same as a branded drug but sold for a much lower price (for example, paracetamol is the generic form of Panadol).

**Gini coefficient** A way to measure inequality, usually applied to household income – and comparing it across time and across economies. A Gini score of 0 implies complete equality, meaning that all households have the same income; a score of exactly 1, on the other hand, suggests complete inequality, meaning that one household gets everything. Actual scores lie somewhere in between.

**Global financial crisis** The period of extreme difficulties in **global financial markets** and banking systems between mid-2007 and early 2009.

**Global financial markets** International markets in financial assets, both bonds and shares, and also more liquid assets, such as government bonds.

**Globalisation** A process whereby all types of economic activity increasingly cross national borders. It includes international trade, foreign direct investment and international capital flows.

**Government bonds** These are how a government borrows money – often referred to in the UK as 'gilts'. A bond issued by the government offers the investor who buys it a fixed rate of return over a fixed period of time, after which the government repays the money, possibly refinancing it by issuing another bond. These bonds are usually regarded as a very low-risk investment and can be easily traded in the bond market.

**Government budget** See **budget deficit**, **budget surplus**.

**Gross domestic product (GDP)** The value of all final goods and services produced in an economy. It is used as the main measure of output and economic activity. However, it excludes most of the output of unpaid work. 'Nominal' GDP is not adjusted for inflation, while 'real' GDP is.

**'Great Moderation'** The period preceding the 2008 financial crisis, when it was claimed that the business cycle had finally been conquered.

**'Great Recession'** The period following the 2008 financial crisis.

**Growth** See **GDP growth**.

**Hedge fund** A fund with looser rules on investor protection, and hence usually for those who are more experienced investors and prepared to accept more risk. They are called 'hedge funds' since they were originally used by investors to 'hedge' their bets, by covering riskier investments with safer ones – usually oil futures.

**Heterodox economics** Any school of economic or social thought (such as post-Keynesian, structuralist, Austrian, Marxian, feminist or institutionalist economics) that provides alternative ideas to those of the currently dominant neoclassical school of economics, which is usually referred to as 'mainstream'.

**Housing equity** The stake (net of any mortgage debt) that a property owner has in their housing.

**Human capital** A person's potential that can augment their productivity and earnings, mostly the product of training, education and experience.

**Income tax (basic, higher and marginal rate)** Tax paid on income. The basic rate of income tax is paid on the lowest taxable incomes, and higher rates are paid by those who earn more. A person's marginal rate of tax is the rate they would incur on an additional pound of income. It will be the rate of tax paid on the top slice of a person's income, which in a progressive income tax system will increase as income rises, with those on higher incomes being taxed at a higher marginal *rate* than those on lower incomes.

**Indirect tax** See **tax (indirect)**.

**Industrial ecosystem** The network of resources that allows companies and industrial sectors to be set up and grow. It includes everything from finance, supply chains, training and help with exporting to changes in the legal rules that would allow smaller companies to cooperate more effectively.

**Industrial policy** Policies intended to support the development of industry, to boost productivity, provide higher-paid jobs, and improve international competitiveness. These policies can include investment in particular industries, tariffs, export incentives, training and technology support policies.

**Inequality** There are many different inequalities, for example, in rates of employment, pay or household income across many different groups, such as between men and women or different ethnic groups. What is generally meant by just 'inequality' is how unequal the distribution of household income is, which can be measured by the Gini coefficient.

**Inflation** The rate at which prices in an economy increase over time. It is measured by price indices such as the **Consumer Price Index** (CPI). While inflation has had a bad press in Britain over the years, you can have too little of it, as well as too much. Deflation, the opposite of inflation, is regarded as especially damaging, since it typically slows consumption and has a highly negative effect on GDP growth.

**Informal care** Care that is provided unpaid by friends or family members.

**Infrastructure** The capital assets of an economy that make possible all its economic and social activity, including both physical infrastructure, such as roads and the internet, and social infrastructure, such as education and care systems. Both types of infrastructure tend to be at least partially paid for by public spending, because their benefits accrue to more than their direct users, who would not, and often could not, pay the costs of their full benefits to society.

**Intellectual property** Capital assets that consist of ideas and knowledge.

**Interest** Regular payments that have to be made paid to borrow money.

**International Monetary Fund (IMF)** An international financial institution established after the Second World War, with the goal of regulating and stabilising financial relationships among countries, and ensuring the free flow of finance around the world economy. Based in Washington, DC, it is governed by a system that grants disproportionate influence to the wealthier economies.

**Keynesian economics** The economics inspired by John Maynard Keynes, who, among many other things, recognised the importance of analysing whether an economy could generate enough demand to achieve full employment, and that expectations about economic prospects, what he called 'animal spirits', would have a key role in this. This is in contrast to the neoclassical school, which focuses more on long-run supply rather than shorter-run demand issues. Keynes famously remarked that in the long run we are all dead. Neoclassical economics also tends towards the idea that there are absolute laws governing economics, which leave room for expectations only if they can be expressed in mathematical laws.

**Labour market** How workers find employment. The sellers in this market are those who are seeking jobs and buyers are potential employers.

**Labour-intensive** A production process that requires particularly large amounts of labour relative to capital.

**Leveraging** Increasing the proportion of debt as a proportion of a company's assets. De-leveraging means paying down debt. A leveraged form of investment is when debt is used to make an investment, for example, buying a company, and, in the case of a company, that debt is then a part of its (leveraged) assets.

**Limited liability** This allows shareholders to limit their commitment to a business to the value of their initial investment in its shares of stock. It is often argued that this also tends to limit their interest in its activities, making room for some fairly questionable activities on the part of management due to a lack of shareholder oversight.

**Liquidity** How easily an asset can be sold for money. Only money itself is wholly liquid, but some assets, such as government bonds, can be easily sold. Fixed assets such as buildings and machinery are some of the least liquid.

**Macroeconomics** The study of aggregate economic indicators such as gross domestic product (GDP), its growth, employment, unemployment and inflation. Conventional economics makes a distinction between macroeconomics and microeconomics (the study of individual businesses or households).

**Macro-prudential regulation** An approach to financial regulation aimed at reducing 'systemic risk', that is, risk to the financial system as a whole.

**Marketisation** Involving private sector companies in the provision of previously public services. This can happen through the state directly contracting out services to private firms or by giving users budgets to spend themselves. When it refers to whole industries it is usually called **privatisation**.

**Means-tested benefits** Payments by the state to eligible individuals and households that depend on household income. Means testing has been argued to be a highly demeaning process, in some cases limiting uptake and undermining the potential effectiveness of such benefits to achieve their aims.

**Microeconomics** The study of the economic behaviour of what are treated as individual 'agents' such as companies, workers and households.

**Minimum wage** A legally imposed minimum wage rate per hour. In the UK, workers aged 25 and over must be paid the so-called 'National Living Wage'. However, this is really just another name for the minimum wage, since its level is not calculated according to the cost of living and is not enough to pay for what is agreed to be a decent standard of living.

**Modelling** Drawing an abstract picture of an economy, or part of it, by making simplifying assumptions to allow a clearer understanding of fundamental processes. Modelling is also necessary in order to apply quantitative analysis and make predictions. Particular models can be criticised for ignoring important processes, but any model needs to make some assumptions.

**Monetary policy** Government agencies, especially the Central Bank, using interest rate adjustments and banking regulation to attempt to control the creation of new credit by the private sector and hence the rate of both economic growth and job creation. 'Tight' (contractionary) monetary policy aims to reduce new credit creation with higher interest rates, while 'loose' (expansionary) policy tries to foster more credit and lending.

**Mortgage** A loan taken out to purchase residential or commercial property. It is secured on the property that can be sold by the lender if the loan conditions are not met.

**Multiplier** A stimulus designed to boost production and employment through government expenditure, resulting in a total increase in spending in the economy that is greater than the original expenditure. This is the multiplier in action and it works because those whose incomes have been increased by the initial expenditure spend some of their increased incomes. Its strength depends on many factors, such as the form of initial spending, how much people save rather than spend, the scale of imports, and the amount of spare capacity in the economy – all of which make the multiplier very hard to calculate in advance. The multiplier also works in the opposite direction. If austerity, rather than stimulus, is applied, the economy will shrink by more than the cut in spending.

**Mutual fund** A fund that pools investments in the shares of many publicly traded companies, to reduce both risk and the overheads of investing in individual corporate shares. An investor buys one or more units in the fund, earning a percentage of the overall income.

**Mutual society** An organisation owned by its members for mutual benefit. Profits are usually reinvested, rather than being paid out, as they would be to shareholders. The precise workings will depend on the purpose of the society. The original 'building' societies, which emerged in 19th-century England to provide housing for ordinary people, were mutual societies, very few of which resisted de-mutualisation during the 1980s.

**National debt** See **public debt**.

**National Development Bank** A bank created by government to provide funding for the country's economic development.

**Natural monopoly** A sector where strong economies of scale are inevitable so that competition will, without preventative regulation, tend to result in the dominance of one supplier. To prevent this, governments tend to regulate or nationalise natural monopolies, including transport infrastructure and public utilities.

**Negative equity** When the amount an asset is worth is less than the outstanding debts incurred in owning it (see **equity**).

**Neoclassical economics** Currently the dominant school of economics. It is both taught and practised worldwide and is especially dominant in countries like the UK, USA, Australia and Ireland. It is used to justify free market economies, by showing that a competitive economy will ensure that all available resources are fully utilised, and that everyone's income is related to their productivity.

**Neoliberalism** A set of political ideas that became dominant globally from the early 1980s in response to the economic problems of the 1970s. Neoliberal policies have emphasised deregulation (including of labour and financial markets), privatisation, globalisation and strict monetary policy. There is also a strong tendency to rely on theoretical models based on neoclassical economics, rather than the evidence of economic history and current events. Neoliberalism has resulted in the current economic situation of both the UK and much of the rest of the world.

**Non-profit institution** An institution whose primary purpose is something other than the making of a profit that reinvests any profits it does make.

**Organisation for Economic Co-operation and Development (OECD)** Set up in 1961, with the objective of helping to promote economic progress and world trade. It has a wider support base than, for example, the G20 (the group of the 20 richest economies), being supported by 36 member countries, and is based in Paris.

**Outsourcing** The process by which firms or the state buy in services from other private contractors (see also **marketisation**).

**Patent monopoly** A form of regulation of intellectual property rights to enable profit to be made from new inventions. An innovation that is patented cannot be used for a specified period of time by those who do not own the patent. Patents are supposed to protect those who have paid for an innovation's development costs and risks, but can be bought and sold.

**Perfect markets/competition** The most competitive market imaginable, in which no individual buyer or seller can influence market conditions or prices by their own actions. Perfectly competitive markets and competition do not, in practice, exist.

**Pensions (occupational, private, state)** An occupational pension scheme is provided by an employer, rather than one taken out privately. The state pension is paid by the state to all eligible retirees.

**Poverty** Poverty can be measured in *absolute* or *relative* terms. A household without the resources to reach a defined minimum standard of living is in 'absolute' poverty. Relative poverty is when the resources available to a household are too low relative to the income of the rest of the population, as measured by, for example, median income. People are classified as being in poverty if their household is, even though households are known not to share resources equally.

**Price elasticity** A measure of how much the amount people buy of a good responds to a change in its price.

**Private equity** A form of business in which the company's entire equity base is owned by one or a small group of individual investors. A private equity company does not issue shares onto the stock market, and hence is not usually required to release public financial statements or comply with other securities regulations. Private equity firms are generally considered to be more ruthlessly focused on generating shorter-term cash profits from their operations than companies listed on the stock market.

**Privatisation** The selling of state-owned assets to private investors. In the UK, a wave of privatisations since the 1980s has included the railway system, public utilities, public housing and even the Royal Mail.

**Productivity** Measures the efficiency of production, in amount produced per worker or per hour of work. Physical productivity measures the physical amount produced, but measurement is more usually in terms of the value produced.

**Progressive/regressive policies** Policies that decrease (regressive) or increase (regressive) income inequality.

**Progressive taxation** See **tax system**.

**Public debt (national debt)** This is made up of the combined deficits of previous years. Much has been made of the supposedly perilous level of this debt in Britain since the 2008 financial crisis. But, while some have claimed that there will be dire effects on economic growth if debt is more than 90 per cent of GDP, they have had less to say when explaining how countries such as Japan appear to be able to happily support debt of 240 per cent of GDP.

**Public/private good** A public good is one that has public benefits, that is, necessarily benefits others than its direct consumers. A private good benefits its direct consumers alone. Public goods are underprovided unless the state pays for them (at least partially), because direct consumers will pay only for their benefits to themselves and not for their wider public benefits.

**Public investment** See **capital account**.

**Publicly Listed Company (PLC)** A company whose shares of stock are owned by a large number of widely dispersed shareholders, and are tradable on a stock market.

**Public procurement** The state buying goods and services it needs (see also **outsourcing**).

**Quantitative easing (QE)** This involves the Central Bank buying large amounts of (often government) bonds from financial institutions – effectively making them far more cash-rich. Although intended as an expansionary policy by raising asset prices and driving down interest rates, its main effects were to support the banks that were damaged during the 2008 crisis, to increase inequality by making asset holders richer, and to produce a stock market boom. In practice, there was very little expansion of the real economy.

**Quasi-market** A sort of market set up within the public sector version of a free market, supposedly to provide the 'benefits' of free market efficiency while preserving the traditional, existing processes of public sector management and ownership. The track record of the NHS's 'internal' market, however, suggests that this idea is not without its problems.

**Real economy** The section of the economy that produces actual goods and services, rather than just financial trading.

**Recession (slump)** The technical definition of a recession is when the total real GDP of an economy shrinks for two or more consecutive quarters.

**Recovery** The opposite of a recession – when GDP has begun to grow again. However, given the optimistic nature of politicians and economists, only one quarter of positive growth is required to constitute a recovery, whereas a recession requires two of negative growth. Recession and recovery are two phases of the economic or 'business' cycle.

**Regulation** A framework of rules and regulations that a sector must adhere to. Regulation is instituted by the government, but the specific rules are often designed, administered and, where necessary, enforced by an independent body, set up for that purpose, usually in the public sector.

**Rentier** An individual or organisation whose income is derived from interest on loans, rents from property and so on.

**Retail banking** See **banking (retail)**.

**Securitisation** A process that converts the flow of income arising from financial commitments (such as loans or credit card debt) into financial assets (such as bonds), which can then be traded in markets.

**Slump** See **contraction** or **recession**.

**Social capital** The strengths of institutions and relationships in a society are sometimes called its social capital.

**Social infrastructure** Infrastructure that consists of 'human and social capital', that is, wealth that resides in the capabilities of individuals and institutions of society and supports the quality of life of a country, region, city or neighbourhood.

This use is in contrast to that of some mainstream economists who would recognise only physical community assets such as schools, universities, hospitals, prisons and community housing as social infrastructure (by our definition, a type of physical infrastructure), but not the systems for the provision of education, health or social services within such buildings.

**Social insurance** A system in which people are compulsorily insured by the state for risks such as sickness, unemployment, etc.

**Social mobility** The ease or difficulty of people moving between socioeconomic strata and escaping or replicating the fortunes of their parents.

**Social prescribing** Prescribing non-medical treatments, such as gym or social club membership, to improve health and wellbeing.

**Social security system** A government system that provides monetary assistance to people according to their needs. It is sometimes pejoratively and misleadingly referred to as 'welfare', to suggest that it provides just hand-outs for a section of the population, rather being a system into which we all pay and also require at various times in our lives.

**Socioeconomic gradient** How access to the good things in life varies with socioeconomic status.

**Sovereign wealth fund** A state-owned investment fund or entity that is commonly established from balance of payments surpluses, official foreign currency operations, the proceeds of privatisations, governmental transfer payments, fiscal surpluses, and/or receipts resulting from resource exports. Despite having been an oil and gas exporter in the 1980s, the UK has no sovereign wealth fund.

**Speculation** Buying in anticipation of a price rise, or selling in anticipation of a price fall. Speculation is at the core of what has been described as 'casino capitalism'. It essentially involves betting on a particular financial outcome. 'Short selling', for example, means betting that a particular company's share will fall in value in a specified, but 'short', period of time.

**State-owned corporation (state-owned enterprise)** A business that is either wholly or partially owned and operated by the government.

**Supply** The amount of a good or service available at any particular price.

**Surplus** See **budget surplus**.

**Sustainability** When what is done in the present does not compromise the ability of future generations to do the same.

**Tariff** A tax imposed on imports, usually to support domestic production of the product in question by making imported goods more expensive.

**Tax (direct)** A tax levied on the income or profits of a person or firm who pays it, rather than on goods or services, like income tax and corporation tax.

**Tax (indirect)** A tax, usually on goods and services, that is paid indirectly by the seller, like VAT or fuel duty.

**Tax avoidance** Taking full advantage of the way the legal system in an economy works to minimise tax liabilities. This is not illegal.

**Tax credits** Benefits paid to low-income families with children and/or in employment. They are means-tested on household income.

**Tax evasion** This involves misrepresenting financial assets and income to save tax and is illegal.

**Tax system (progressive, regressive, flat rate)** A progressive income tax system taxes people at a higher rate the more they earn, while in a regressive system the rate decreases as people earn more. A flat rate system is one where everyone pays the same tax rate, regardless of their income.

**Transaction costs** Costs incurred during the process of buying or selling that are not the inherent cost of providing a good or service. Policy-makers often claim that their policies will reduce transactions costs.

**Unemployment** Individuals who would like to be employed, and are actively seeking employment, but cannot find a job are considered 'officially' unemployed. Individuals who are not employed but not actively looking for employment, even if they are doing unpaid caring work, are considered to be outside of the labour force and hence don't count as unemployed.

**Unemployment rate** The number of unemployed people measured as a proportion of the labour force.

**Universal Basic Income (UBI)** A system under which all adults, regardless of their income, employment status, wealth, marital status or any other circumstances receive an income from the government intended to cover the basic cost of living (also known as Citizen's Income).

**Universal Credit (UC)** A **means-tested benefit** aimed at people of working age who are either looking for work or earn a low income. It replaces a number of previous means-tested benefits and tax credits by a single monthly payment, which has caused considerable hardship and increased the use of food banks. Its introduction has been considerably delayed.

**Universalism/means testing** Universal benefits are based on social solidarity and paid at the same rate to all eligible claimants. Means-tested benefits are targeted and paid at a level that depends on a claimant's household income. In recent years, governments have tended to favour means testing, moving away from the principle of universalism.

**Wealth tax** A tax in which owners of wealth, or particular forms of wealth (such as financial wealth, real estate or inheritances), must pay a specified proportion of that wealth to the government, usually on an annual basis.

**World Bank (The)** An international financial organisation formed after the Second World War and based in Washington, DC. Its supposed goal is to promote the economic development of poor regions of the world through subsidised loans, economic advice and other forms of assistance. In practice, it has played an important role in reinforcing neoliberal economic policies in developing countries, including through the aggressive use of conditionality strategies, that make development assistance dependent on conforming to rules specified by the Bank.

**World Trade Organization (WTO)** An international economic organisation formed in 1995 and based in Geneva, Switzerland, which is dedicated to promoting greater trade and investment among its members. Most countries in the world now belong to the WTO, and hence have committed to reducing tariffs on imports, reducing non-tariff barriers to trade, reducing restrictions on foreign investment, and generally following a pro-market vision of economic development.

**Zero-hours contracts** Employment contracts with no guaranteed hours. Employees are not guaranteed any work by their employers (and therefore no pay).

# References and further reading

Adams, R. (2018) 'Teachers warn of growing poverty crisis in British schools', *The Guardian,* 2 April, www.theguardian.com/education/2018/apr/02/teachers-warn-of-growing-poverty-crisis-in-british-schools

Amountzias, V., Dagdeviren, H. and Patokos, T. (2017) 'A waste of energy? A critical assessment of the investigation of the UK energy market by the CMA', *Competition and Change* 21, 1.

Amountzias, V., Dagdeviren, H. and Patokos, T. (2017) 'Pricing decisions and market power in the UK electricity market', *Energy Policy* 108, 8.

Andreoni, A. (2016) 'Varieties of industrial policy: Models, packages and transformation cycles', in A. Noman and J. Stiglitz (eds) *Efficiency, Finance and Varieties of Industrial Policy,* New York: Columbia University Press, 245–305.

Andreoni, A. and Chang, H.-J. (2018) 'The political economy of industrial policy: Structural interdependencies, policy alignment and conflict management', *Structural Change and Economic Dynamics* 48, 136–50, https://doi.org/10.1016/j.strueco.2018.10.007

Atkinson, A.B. (2015) *Inequality,* Cambridge, MA: Harvard University Press.

Autenne, A., Biondi, Y., Cavalier, G., Cotiga, A., Doralt, P., Haslam, C. et al (2018) *The Current Challenges for EU Company and Financial Law and Regulation Business and Financial Law,* Green Paper, Vienna: SIG of the European Law Institute (ELI), 2 January, https://goo.gl/KKVUEk

Baker, D. (2016) *Rigged: How Globalization and the Rules of the Modern Economy Are Structured to Make the Richer,* https://deanbaker.net/books/rigged.htm

Barr, B., Higgerson, J. and Whitehead, M. (2017) 'Investigating the impact of the English health inequalities strategy: Time trend analysis', *BMJ* 358, j3310.

Barr, B., Taylor-Robinson, D., Scott-Samuel, A., McKee, M. and Stuckler, D. (2012) 'Suicides associated with the 2008 10 economic recession in England: time trend analysis', *BMJ* 345.

Boskin Commission (1996) *The Boskin Commission Report*, www. ssa.gov/history/reports/boskinrpt.html

British Academy (2014) *'If You Could Do One Thing...' Nine Local Actions to Reduce Health Inequalities*, www.thebritishacademy. ac.uk/publications/if-you-could-do-one-thing

Buchan, I., Kontopantelis, E., Sperrin, M. Chandola, T. and Doran, T. (2017) 'North–South disparities in English mortality 1965–2015: Longitudinal population study', *Journal of Epidemiology and Community Health* doi:10.1136/jech-201-209195.

Cameron, D. (2009) 'The age of austerity', Speech, 26 April, https://conservative-speeches.sayit.mysociety.org/ speech/601367

Clery, E., Curtice, J. and Harding, R. (2017) *British Social Attitudes 34*, London: NatCen, www.bsa.natcen.ac.uk/ media/39196/bsa34_full-report_fin.pdf

Cozzi, G. Bargawi, H. and Himmelweit, S. (eds) (2016) *Economics and Austerity in Europe: Gendered Impacts and Sustainable Alternatives*, London: Routledge.

Cruddas, J. and Kibasi, T. (2016) 'A universal basic mistake', *Prospect Magazine*, June.

De Henau, J. (2019) *Employment and Fiscal Effects of Investing in Universal Childcare: A Macro-micro Simulation Analysis for the UK*, Open University IKD Working Paper No 83, www.open. ac.uk/ikd/publications/working-papers/83

Downes, A. and Lansley, S. (eds) (2018) *It's Basic Income, The Global Debate*, Bristol: Policy Press.

Exworthy, M., Mannion, R. and Powell, M. (eds) (2016) *Dismantling the NHS? Evaluating the Impact of Health Reforms*, Bristol: Policy Press.

Fabian Society (2014) *A Convenient Truth: A Better Society for Us and the Planet by Richard Wilkinson and Kate Pickett*, Fabian Ideas 638, www.fabians.org.uk/wp-content/uploads/2014/09/A-Convenient-Truth.pdf

Ghilarducci, T., Fisher, B. and Knauss, Z. (2015) *Now Is the Time to Add Retirement Accounts to Social Security: The Guaranteed Retirement Account Proposal*, New York: Schwartz Center for Economic Policy Research, The New School.

Green, F. and Kynaston, D. (2019) *Engines of Privilege: Britain's Private School Problem*, London: Bloomsbury.

Green, F., Dorling, D. and Minton, J. (2017) 'The geography of a rapid rise in elderly mortality in England and Wales, 2014–15', *Health & Place* 44, 77–85.

Hills, J. (2017) *Good Times, Bad Times: The Welfare Myth of Them and Us*, Bristol: Policy Press.

Inman, P. (2018) 'Household debt in UK "worse than any time on record"', *The Guardian,* 26 July, www.theguardian.com/money/2018/jul/26/household-debt-in-uk-worse-than-at-any-time-on-record

Institute for Health Equity (2017) *Life Expectancy Rises 'Grinding to Halt'*, UCL Institute of Epidemiology and Health Care, www.ucl.ac.uk/iehc/iehc-news/michael-marmot-life-expectancy

Konzelmann, S. (2014) *The Economics of Austerity*, Cheltenham: Edward Elgar.

Konzelmann, S. (2019) *Austerity*, Cambridge: Polity Press.

Konzelmann, S. and Fovargue-Davies, M. (2016) 'Public Policy Working: Catalyst for Olympic Success', in G. Cozzi, S. Newman and J. Toporowski (eds) *Finance and Industrial Policy: Beyond Financial Regulation in Europe*, Oxford: Oxford University Press, 140–61.

Konzelmann, S. and Fovargue-Davies, M. (2017) *Time to Stop Playing Games with Industrial Policy? What Government and Business Might Learn from Team GB*, Centre for Business Research Working Paper No 488, Cambridge: University of Cambridge, March.

Konzelmann, S., Fovargue-Davies, M. and Wilkinson, F. (2018) 'Britain's industrial evolution: The structuring role of economic theory', *Journal of Economic Issues* 52, 1, 1–30.

Konzelmann, S., Deakin, S., Fovargue-Davies, M. and Wilkinson, F. (2018) *Labour, Finance and Inequality: The Insecurity Cycle in British Public Policy*, London: Routledge.

Labour Party, 'A More Equal Society' manifesto, https://labour.org.uk/manifesto/a-more-equal-society/

Lansley, S. (2016) *A Sharing Economy: How Social Wealth Funds Can Reduce Inequality and Balance the Books*, Bristol: Policy Press.

Lansley, S. and Reed, H. (2019) *Basic Income for All: From Desirability to Feasibility*, Pireas, Greece: Compass.

Lansley, S., McCann, D. and Schifferes, S. (2018) *Remodelling Capitalism: How Social Wealth Funds Could Transform Britain*, York: Friends Provident Foundation.

Le Grand, J., Mays, N. and Mulligan, J. (eds) (1998) *Learning from the NHS Internal Market: A Review of the Evidence*, London: King's Fund.

Mays, N., Jones, L. and Dixon, A. (eds) (2011) *Understanding New Labour's Market Reforms of the English NHS*, London: King's Fund.

Mackenbach, J.P. (2010) 'Has the English strategy to reduce health inequalities failed?', *Social Science & Medicine* 71, 7, 1249–53.

Macintyre, S. (1999) 'Reducing health inequalties: An action report', *Critical Public Health*, 9(4), 347–50.

Marmot, M. (2010) *Fair Society, Healthy Lives: Strategic Review of Health Inequalities in England post-2010*, London: HM Government.

Monbiot, G. et al (2019) *Land for the Many*, The Labour Party.

Montgomerie, J. (2019) *Should We Abolish Household Debts?*, Cambridge: Polity.

Mutuals Taskforce (2012) *Public Service Mutuals: The Next Steps*, London: Cabinet Office.

NHS England (2014) *Five Year Forward View*, London: NHS England.

Onaran, Ö. (2018) 'Public Investment in Social Infrastructure for a Caring, Sustainable and Productive Economy', in J. McDonnell (ed) *Economics for the Many*, London: Verso, 186–94.

Onaran, Ö. and Tori, D. (2017) *Productivity Puzzle? Financialization, Inequality, Investment in the UK*, GPERC Policy Briefs, University of Greenwich.

Onaran, Ö., Nikolaidi, M. and Obst, T. (2017) *The Role of Public Spending and Incomes Policies for Investment and Equality-led Development in the UK*, GPERC Policy Briefs, University of Greenwich.

Osborne, G. (2010) 'A new economic model', Mais Lecture, 24 February, https://conservative-speeches.sayit.mysociety.org/speech/601526

Parker, G. (2016) 'Veteran of Treasury battles tots up a decade's wins and losses', *Financial Times*, 14 April, www.ft.com/content/295dd92e-ff21-11e5-99cb-83242733f755

Reed, H. and Lansley, S. (2016) *A Universal Basic Income, An Idea Whose Time Has Come?*, Compass, www.compassonline.org.uk/publications/universal-basic-income-an-idea-whose-time-has-come/

Schrecker, T. and Bambra, C. (2015) *How Politics Makes Us Sick: Neoliberal Epidemics*, London: Palgrave Macmillan.

Schuller, T. and Watson, D. (2009) *Learning through Life: Inquiry into the Future of Lifelong Learning*, Leicester: National Institute of Adult Continuing Education.

Seery, E. (2014) *Working for the Many: Public Services Fight Inequality*, Oxfam Briefing Paper 182, https://policy-practice.oxfam.org.uk/publications/working-for-the-many-public-services-fight-inequality-314724

Singh, M. (2018) 'Poll shows even Tory voters feel austerity has gone too far', *Financial Times*, 2 May.

Skidelsky, R. and Fraccaroli, N. (2017) *Austerity vs Stimulus: The Political Future of Economic Recovery*, London: Palgrave Macmillan.

Smith, J. (2017) 'The Karl Polanyi 1940 Bennington Lecture series in one go', www.primeeconomics.org/articles/the-1940-polanyi-bennington-lectures-series-in-one-go

Smith K.E. and Kandlik Eltanani, M. (2015) 'What kinds of policies to reduce health inequalities in the UK do researchers support?', *Journal of Public Health* 37, 1, 6–17.

Smith, K.E., Bambra, C. and Hill, S.E. (2016) *Health Inequalities: Critical Perspectives*, Oxford: Oxford University Press.

Taylor-Robinson, D. and Barr, B. (2017) 'Death rate now rising in UK's poorest infants', *BMJ* 357, j2258.

WBG (Women's Budget Group) (2016) *Investing in the Care Economy – A Gender Analysis of Employment Stimulus in Seven OECD Countries*, www.ituc-csi.org/investing-in-the-care-economy

WBG (2017) *Investing in the Care Economy: Stimulating Employment Affects by Gender in Countries in Emerging Economies*, London: WBG, https://wbg.org.uk/analysis/investing-care-emerging-economies

Weeks, J. (2018) 'Same old same old … Tory austerity', Prime Blog, 15 May, www.primeeconomics.org/articles/same-old-same-oldtory-austerity

Wilkinson, R. and Pickett, K. (2014) *A Convenient Truth: A Better Society for Us and the Planet*, Fabian Ideas 638, Fabian Society Report.

Work and Pensions Committee (2018) *Report on Collective Defined Contribution Pension Schemes*, www.parliament.uk/business/committees/committees-a-z/commons-select/work-and-pensions-committee/inquiries/parliament-2017/collective-pension-schemes-17-19

# Index